Awake: The Return of Men

Joseph King

Published by New Nationalists
New York, 2018

The Return of Men

Other books by Joseph King

Awake: An Introduction to New Nationalism

Joseph King

Contents

The Return of Men

Introduction

Ida Tarbell was a leading journalist in the early twentieth century and, for most of her life, a devout feminist. In her later years, her faith in feminism moderated and her view on women changed. In 1912, almost a decade before the 19th Amendment granted universal suffrage, she wrote, "Men and women are widely apart in functions and in possibilities. They cannot be made equal by exterior devices like trousers, ballots, the study of Greek."[1]

In August of 2017, an engineer at Google wrote a balanced and well-researched memo speculating that there were proportionately fewer women in the tech industry in part because of biological differences between men and women.[2] He cited a number of research articles showing that, on average, there seem to be fundamental differences between the sexes. For example, men tend to be more interested in things while women tend to be more interested in people. These differences, he reasoned, could help explain why there were fewer female en-

---

[1] Ida Tarbell. *The Business of Being a Woman* (New York: MacMillan, 1912), 213.

[2] Kate Conger, "Exclusive: Here's The Full 10-Page Anti-Diversity Screed Circulating Internally at Google," Gizmodo, August 5, 2017, accessed April 26, 2018, https://gizmodo.com/exclusive-heres-the-full-10-page-anti-diversity-screed-1797564320

gineers in Silicon Valley than male engineers. Women, by nature, were simply less interested in engineering.[3]

James Damore's thoughtful memo was internally circulated within Google as a critique of Google's aggressive affirmative action policies, which simply assumed the lower representation of women in engineering roles was due to sex discrimination. His memo eventually found its way to the public, where it generated a wave of outrage that dominated the news cycle for days. Editorial after editorial across all major publications tried to outdo one another in expressing their condemnation of Damore's "sexist" and "backward" views. A number of scientists affirmed that Damore's scientific evidence was sound, but that didn't matter to the media.[4] They were appalled at the suggestion that men and women were, on average, different.

I grew up believing that men and women were essentially the same. I believed the sexes were largely

[3] Tarbell, 37. Tarbell also noted over a century earlier in the same book that "[women] will show less enthusiasm for technical problems, for machinery and engineering, more for social problems, particularly when it is a question of meeting them with preventives or remedies."
[4] Lee Jussim, "The Google Memo: Four Scientists Respond," *Quillette,* August 7, 2017, accessed April 26, 2018, http://quillette.com/2017/08/07/google-memo-four-scientists-respond/

products of socialization, and cheered the movement towards higher representation of women across fields. Those were the beliefs instilled in me by the school system, and re-enforced by the mainstream media. But the more life experience I gained, the more I began to realize that there were very real and sizable differences between men and women in many areas. My awareness set me on a course that began in earnest curiosity into what these differences were, but ended in fundamentally changing my worldview.

The current mainstream view of equality between the sexes is a significant historical anomaly. The norm since the dawn of civilization, and across all cultures, is to recognize different roles for men and women. In Western civilization, there were clear ideas of what it meant to be a man, and clear ideas of what it meant to be a woman. Roughly speaking, men were to be brave, strong, and responsible heads of households. They provided for their family and worked with other men to protect their community from external threats. Women were to be nurturing mothers who cared for children and managed the home. These roles were partly due to socialization, but also a reflection of basic differences between the sexes that are grounded in biology.

The sexes approach the world differently, because on average they are different. These differences are the result of the very different reproductive problems men and women have faced throughout our evolutionary history. For a man to be reproductively successful meant for him to defend his tribe and outcompete other men for access to as many women as possible. On the other hand, a woman faces a different reproductive problem. Unlike a man, she bears a higher cost of reproduction due to a lengthy pregnancy term, which limits the amount of children she can have. A woman is reproductively successful if she can keep the children she has alive, which was difficult in a world without hospitals or supermarkets. Because each sex faced a different reproductive problem, sexual selection has, over time, carved out distinct feminine and masculine human natures. Men are born to be warriors, and women are born to be mothers. These are the roles etched in our biology and that we've played throughout history.

In recent decades, a small but vocal group of people have fought to destroy these gender roles. They claim such roles are discriminatory, and assert that women and men are equal in all aspects. Some go so far as to suggest that women are physically weaker than men simply because of socialization. The logical conclusion of these beliefs is a world where half the engineers, scientists, executives, and even soldiers are women. When these radicals don't observe this in real life, they claim the world is sexist. The ultimate conclusion of their efforts is a world where there are no longer any women, just males and female men. This is the view of modern feminists.

Cracks in the ideology of these feminists are readily apparent in real life. For example, a visit to any university will reveal that women are much more interested in the arts, humanities, and nursing than they are in math, science, and engineering. Any parent can tell you that their daughters try to have conversations with their toys, while their sons turn every toy into a weapon. Any elementary school boy can tell you that girls cry much more easily than boys do. These observations are not culture specific; they are observed throughout the world. Women are not the same as men, and the differences matter.

The consequences of feminism have been disastrous for our nation. Many feminists have found their way into positions of authority in academia, which, in recent decades, has been a hotbed of radicalism. From that vantage point, they raised entire generations in the doctrine of feminism. Their results are readily apparent: divorce rates have skyrocketed, male participation in the labor force is at multi-year lows, the percent of children born to single mothers is over 40%, and the life satisfaction of women today is lower than prior generations. The days of children growing up in stable households on home cooked meals are all but over. The modern woman is taught that homemaking is degrading, and that, instead, she should strive for a high powered career. As a result, the social fabric of our nation is disintegrating.

Until the last century, men ruled the world. Indeed, all of civilization was built in the image of man. Nations were hierarchal, rule based, and aggressive. History was a story of groups of men banding together to fight other groups of men. This all changed with the granting of universal suffrage and the emergence of a feminist conscience. For the first time in the course of history, women now have a large role in national affairs. This has led to the rise of empathy as an important consideration in policy and driven our politics steadily leftward. It seems the government has become, in many ways, a surrogate husband, providing food, shelter, health care, and any number of free services to the public. Our public discourse now has a greater emphasis on emotion and perception rather than sound argument. There is now also a relentless effort towards an inclusive society in which everyone feels welcome and no one's feelings are hurt.

There hasn't been a single nation in the history of the world built by women. A glance of the policies pushed by feminists reveals why. If feminists ruled the nation, we would have everything paid for by the government, we would open our borders to all the world's poor, and we would throw people who said mean things in jail. If feminists ruled, our nation would descend into madness until collapsing under the weight of public debt and boundless illegal immigration. Thankfully, while feminists are ascendant, they're not yet triumphant.

The success of feminism is in large part due to a mass censorship of truth on the different natures of men and women. These facts are silenced by an aggressive minority of "politically correct" ideologues who gained control of the public dialogue in large part because of the cowardice of the majority. By hiding this truth, feminists are able to assert their views on an equal basis to men. They are able to spread their views by claiming parity to men in men's traditional leadership roles in public life. But the feminine nature has evolved to take care of a family, not the interests of a broader group of people. Feminist views have no place on the national stage.

A successful challenge to feminism is to affirm the truth and importance of traditional gender roles. These gender roles are apparent throughout history and well-grounded in evolutionary biology and evolutionary psychology. What feminists present as progress in a struggle for women's right is, in fact, a dark age of misinformation. Freedom is not the same as happiness or success. For a man or woman to be happy, they must play the role that is given them by biology. For our nation to be strong, we need men managing national affairs, and women raising families.

Why Are There Differences?

In the early days of Rome, the young city was a growing regional power populated by tough but unsavory characters. Despite the growing prestige and influence of Rome, the Romans had a serious problem: there weren't enough women for all the men. Roman leaders sent envoys to states throughout the region requesting inter-marriage, but all requests were denied. The neighboring states did not want to marry off their daughters to a bunch of thugs. The frustrated Romans came up with a plan: they put on a great celebration and invited all the neighboring people. Once the celebration started and all the guests let their guard down, the Romans leapt forth and seized all the female guests. The Romans kept these women as their wives while the parents of the captured women fled.[5]

Throughout history, men survived by dominating other men as well as women. Women, being physically weaker, couldn't compete directly in a world

---

[5] Titus Livius. *The History of Rome*. Book 1, Chapter 9.

where bands of men constantly fought each other. Men survived by being strong and working together, women survived by being subservient to whomever was in power. When the Nazis took Paris in 1940, thousands of French women married Nazi soldiers even as millions of French men sat in prison camps.[6] When Moses led the Israelis to victory over the Midianites, the Israelis slaughtered every man but took the virgins as spoils of war.[7] Until modern times, life was a brutal struggle for both men and women.

The different circumstances confronting men and women have led to a different set of behaviors for each sex. For example, when there are enemies threatening the community, men go forth and risk their lives in defense of their tribe. When men feel strong, they go forth and conquer other people and take the spoils back to enrich their tribe. Even though many end up dead or injured, men march on either for survival or glory. In contrast, a woman isn't expected to defend her community. A woman

---

[6] Louise Boyle, "Sex and the Stormtroopers: How French Women Fell for the Nazi Invaders During the Second World War, *Daily Mail*. October 3, 2011, accessed April 26, 2018, http://www.dailymail.co.uk/news/article-2044614/Sex-stormtroopers-How-French-women-fell-Nazi-invaders-Second-World-War.html

[7] Numbers 31:18. In Deuteronomy 20:14 Moses explicitly lays out the Israeli rules of war, stating that upon victory, enemy men are to be slaughtered and women taken.

doesn't put her life on the line for anyone but her own children.

A universal feature of all human societies is a division of roles between men and women.[8] In hunter-gatherers, men hunted while women gathered. In traditional Western civilization, women tended the home while men worked outside of the home. Women spent most of their time with other women; they had their own social world with corresponding statuses, responsibilities, and modes of communication. The same could be said for men. Some observers lament this division of roles as the subjugation of women by men, but that would be a terrible simplification. Men and women have simply held different roles, reflecting basic differences between the sexes. Women may not have held as much political power as men, but they had power over other issues such as how children were raised and how money would be spent.

Our contemporary culture has upended the longstanding division of roles by sex. Most people today are taught growing up that women can do everything men can – essentially that they are the same as men. Some go so far as to say that gender is

---

[8] Naomi Quinn. "Anthropological Studies on Women's Status," *Annual Review of Anthropology* 6 (1977), 187, accessed April 26, 2018, https://sites.duke.edu/nquinn/files/2014/10/womenstatus.pdf

a social construct, and observable gender differences are largely a result of an oppressive social system. These people loudly complain about the absence of women among Navy Seals, corporate CEOs, high tech companies, or any other male-dominated industry. They expect women to hold half of the positions across all industries, since women are half of population. While sex discrimination may play a role, the most obvious explanation for discrepancies in sex representation is that men and women on average are different.

On average, men and women differ across a spectrum of physical and psychological traits. Most people intuitively pick this up through life, but the section below will provide a firmer foundation on why this came about. Differences in behavior between the sexes are consistent across cultures, so they cannot purely be a product of socialization but must at least in part be based in biology. Given that men and women faced different survival problems over the course of history, it should be expected that, through sexual selection, they've developed some differences that are more than skin deep.

Sexual Selection
The male orangutan is the classic deadbeat dad. After fathering a child, he disappears into the wil-

derness and plays no part in raising the infant.[9] That responsibility falls to orangutan mothers, who must carefully carry around and nurture the child for the first few years of the child's life. Orangutans are intelligent creatures capable of developing basic tools and transmitting culture through social interaction, but no one would suggest a male orangutan could be socialized to play a greater role in the upbringing of his offspring. Male and female orangutans behave according to their biological programming, like any other animal.

The difference between human behavior and orangutan behavior is a difference of degree. We still come with a set of genetic programming that, in part, determines what we think and how we act. For example, girls born with a genetic condition where their bodies overproduce male hormones show signs of masculinization even in early childhood. Compared to their female siblings and cousins, they prefer to play with toys that boys typically prefer, such as trucks or blocks, rather than toys girls typically prefer such as dolls and kitchen sup-

---

[9] John Allman, "Big Brains and Parenting," *Engineering & Science* 61, no. 4, 1998, 11, accessed April 26, 2018, http://calteches.library.caltech.edu/3964/1/Parenting.pdf

plies.[10] This shows that typical male behavior is in part grounded in biology.

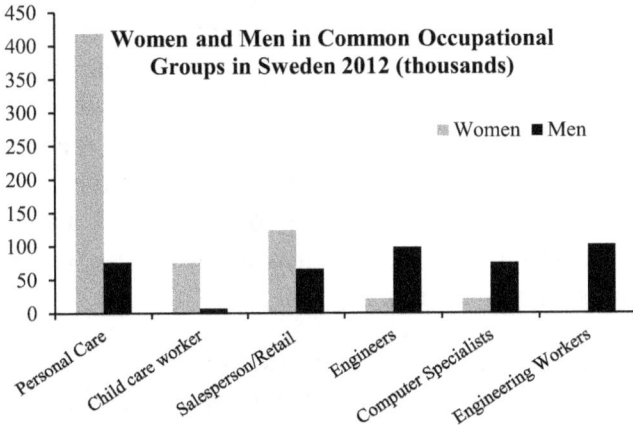

Source: Statistics Sweden, Women and Men in Sweden, 2014

Interestingly, differences between the sexes are actually more apparent the more socially equal the two sexes are. Occupational segregation between the sexes is particularly strong in Scandinavia, which is the most gender egalitarian region in the word. [11] Despite equal educational opportunities, stringent anti-discrimination laws, and a generous welfare system, Swedish men and women volun-

---

[10] Sheri A. Berenbaum and Melissa Hines. "Early Androgens Are Related to Childhood Sex-Typed Toy Preferences," *Psychological Science* 3, no. 3, May 1992, 203-206.

[11] World Economic Forum, *The Global Gender Gap Report*, 2017.

Joseph King

tarily choose very different occupations. Gender
equality provides them with the freedom to pursue
their interests free from social pressure, so men can
pursue male interests and women can pursue female interests. Swedish women tend to end up in
nurturing fields dealing with people, and Swedish
men tend to end up in technical fields dealing with
things. This clearly shows that men and women are
born with different interests, but it doesn't answer
why that's the case. The answer to that question
comes from Darwin.

Natural selection, first proposed by Charles Darwin
in 1859, is one of the most powerful ideas in all of
science. It is able to elegantly explain why we see so
much variation in organisms across the world and
across time. While it explains why species differ, it
does not explain why there are differences between
sexes of the same species. Scientists call this phenomena sexual dimorphism. For example, female
Black Widow spiders are twice as large as male
Black Widow spiders. In humans, some obvious
differences between sexes are seen in average
height and physical strength. Men are, on average,
taller than women in all known human societies.[12]
When it comes to upper body strength, the average

[12] J. Patrick Gray and Linda D. Wolfe. "Height and Sexu-
al Dimorphism of Stature Among Human Societies,"
American Journal of Physical Anthropology 53, no. 3,
September, 1980, 441-456.

man is roughly twice as strong as the average woman is.[13] To explain sexual dimorphism, Darwin proposed an ideal closely related to natural selection: sexual selection.[14]

How does Natural Selection work?

Species adapt to their environments through a process called natural selection. Darwin stumbled upon the idea on a journey to the Galapagos in the 1830s where he intended to observe and document the animals on the island. He noticed that some of the finches on the Galapagos had larger beaks, and some had smaller beaks. The finches with larger beaks were able to eat larger seeds, while those with smaller beaks had to eat smaller seeds. The types of seeds available on the island changed year to year depending on environmental conditions. Darwin noticed that if a season had an abundance of large seeds but fewer small seeds, there would be fewer birds with small beaks in the following year. He reasoned that in times where larger seeds were more abundant, finches with larger beaks were better able to survive and reproduce because their larger beaks made it easier for them to eat the large seeds. On the other hand, birds with smaller beaks

---

[13] Jean Barrett Holloway et al. "Strength Training for Female Athletes: A Position Paper: Part I," *NSCA Journal* 11, no. 4, 1989, 43-51.
[14] Charles Darwin, *The Descent of Man, and Selection in Relation to Sex* (New York: D. Appelton & Co., 1871).

would have trouble eating the larger seeds and many of them would starve. Eventually, the average beak size of the finches would gradually increase because more finches with larger beaks would survive and reproduce than those with smaller beaks. At its core, natural selection depends only on three principles:

First, there are variations within a species. For example, in any group of birds, some are slightly faster than others are.

Second, there is a struggle for survival. Birds are in competition for limited food and must avoid predators. Given this situation, slightly faster birds would have a better chance of beating out other birds to food sources and escaping predators. These faster birds are more likely than slower birds to survive and reproduce.

Third, genetic variations are heritable. A faster bird is more likely to have faster offspring. Since faster birds are more likely to survive and reproduce, then, over generations, more birds will have the genes that allow them to fly faster. Eventually, all the birds in the environment will become faster.

Darwin noticed that peacocks had large, elaborate tails while peahens didn't. This frustrated him, because it seemed that having a large, heavy tail would put the peacock at a disadvantage when it came to avoiding predators. Under his theory of natural selection, large tails would be maladaptive and should have faded from the gene pool, as peacocks with larger tails would be slower and more easily killed by predators. Darwin reconciled this by theorizing that while large tails made peacocks easier prey, they were likely considered attractive to peahens. Perhaps due to nothing more than chance, peahens preferred to mate with peacocks with large tails. The large tails conferred a mating advantage that outweighed its disadvantages. Large-tailed peacocks were thus more reproductively successful, implying that in successive generations, more peacocks would possess the genes for large tails. Over time, the average length of the peacock's tail would then rise. As this type of selection was largely driven by mating preferences, it was called sexual selection.

Sexual selection consists of two components: male-to-male competition and female choice. In female choice competition, females of a species refuse to mate with males that lack certain characteristics. This was the case described above where female peacocks strongly preferred males that have long and beautiful tails, but avoid males that have tails that are relatively short. In male-to-male competition, the males of a species compete with each other for mating opportunities. Males that are larger and stronger have an advantage in these competitions, as they're able to block or kill weaker males. Since the strongest males have the best chance of passing on their genes, over time, the males of species with intense male-to-male competition tend to become larger and stronger relative to the females. Male elephant seals, which are subject to intense male-to-male competition, are two to seven times as large as female elephant seals.[15] The male seals fight one another to establish a dominance hierarchy, where higher ranked males have better access to females. Physical size is a key determinant in the outcome of their fights, so, naturally, larger seals are more likely to pass on their genes.

One might ask how sexual selection can operate, since both females and males share large portions of genes. At times, what's sexually attractive in a man would be unattractive in a woman, and vice versa. For example, women prefer taller men but men prefer shorter women. A tall man may easily find a mate and have sons who are six feet, but also daughters who are six feet. Height would be a reproductive advantage for his sons, but not his daughters. The tall dad might end up with a family of tall daughters who end up unmarried, thus ne-

---

[15] Michael P. Haley, Charles J. Deutsch, and Burney J. Le Boeuf, "Size, Dominance and Copulatory Success in Male Northern Elephant Seals, Mirounga angustirostris," *Animal Behavior* 48, no. 6, December 1994, 1249-1260.

gating the reproductive advantages his height brought him.

Researchers don't yet fully understand the genetic mechanism of how sexual selection operates, but they have a number of ideas.[16] Some traits could be sex-linked, where they only show up on the male sex chromosome and so are only passed on from male to male. Some traits could be expressed differently or even silenced depending on whether the offspring is male or female. The same genes that would lead to a six-foot tall man may be expressed in a more limited extent in a woman, leading her to grow to five feet eight inches. Tall dads tend to have tall sons and daughters, but what is considered tall for a woman is different than that for a man. Under these proposed mechanisms, sexual selection can operate by allowing traits adaptive for males to primarily be passed on to male offspring, and traits adaptive for females to primarily be passed on to female offspring.

---

[16] Russell Bonduriansky, "The Genetic Architecture of Sexual Dimorphism: The Potential Roles of Genomic Imprinting and Condition-Dependence," in *Sex, Size and Gender Roles: Evolutionary Studies of Sexual Size Dimorphism,* ed. Daphne J. Fairbairn, Wolf U. Blanckenhorn, and Tamás Székely (Oxford, England: Oxford University press, 2007), 176-184, accessed April 25, 2018, http://bonduriansky.net/SSGR17.pdf

The two components of sexual selection operate at the same time, though with different degrees of influence, depending on the species. Humans clearly exhibit sexual dimorphism, indicating that we have been subject to sexual selection. While physical differences between men and women are apparent, researchers have also consistently found differences in some psychological traits between the average man and average woman. While some may assert that these psychological differences are cultural, they hold true across human cultures. The universality of the differences suggests a biological, rather than a cultural explanation. In addition, psychological differences between men and women are also clearly seen in early childhood at an age when children are largely free of cultural influence.

Evolutionary psychologists have been very successful in applying principals of sexual selection to understand how these sex differences have emerged. Fundamentally, men and women have faced very different reproductive problems over the course of history. If a woman has sex, she may become pregnant, in which case she must carry a child for ten months and then be responsible for years of childcare. In contrast, for a man, sex has virtually no consequences. A woman is reproductively successful if she successfully raises her children, but a man can be reproductively successful by simply impregnating as many women as he can and leaving child-care to the women.

The different problems men and women face when it comes to reproduction set the stage for sexual selection. Women would be most reproductively successful by adeptly caring for children and choosing a mate who would help protect and provide for her children. This is in line with the traditional notion that men should behave as gentlemen to court women. Men would be most reproductively successful by impregnating as many fertile women as possible. This means becoming a dominant male who is able to keep other rivals at bay. Unsurprisingly, men seek status and power to a much higher degree than women do.

In addition to facing different reproductive problems, men and women have also faced very different survival problems. Survival is a necessary condition to reproduction. In the industrialized world today, we enjoy a high degree of physical safety and abundant food. But for most of history, life was treacherous. Imagine a world without electricity lighting up the streets at night, without a phone to call police when bad guys appear, and without even running water to wash food and wounds. For most of history, the world was a very dangerous place full of violence and disease.

The earliest form of human organization was hunter-gatherers. Humans spent the bulk of their existence as hunter-gatherers, so our genes are most likely best adapted to the hunter-gatherer life-style. Hunter-gatherers are usually a group of about forty related people who live in temporary settlements and forage for food. Like all pre-modern societies, there is a clear division of labor: men hunt wild animals while women gather food and rear children. Starvation was common, so men who were poor hunters would have trouble feeding their families. Child mortality was high, so women who were not closely attentive to their children would lose them to diseases or accidents.

In this broader context, it's easy to see how the different challenges each sex faced could have led to different adaptations. Men, whose survival depends on hunting, need to be physically strong, good at throwing projectiles, and able to work together with other men to track animals. Women, who at the time spent a large part of their reproductive lives pregnant, were more vulnerable and would have benefited from a higher degree of anxiety and risk aversion.

The different reproductive and survival challenges faced by each sex offer a framework to understand why men and women would, on average, have different physical and psychological characteristics.

The basic predictions offered by this framework conform to everyday observations. Men like competitive team activities involving throwing objects, be it a baseball, basketball, football, or cricket ball. Women have significantly less interest in those activities, but prefer maintaining relationships and discussing feelings. The following section will provide a more precise breakdown of differences between the sexes, based on recent scientific research.

Joseph King

The Warrior and the Mother

In 2005, the National Bureau of Economic Research hosted a conference on the representation of women in the natural sciences. Larry Summers, an eminent economist and President of Harvard University at the time, offered a few ideas as to why women may be underrepresented. One of his ideas was based in biology: there may be fewer women in the fields because, on average, there are fewer women interested or sufficiently talented to pursue the fields.[17] This idea, while completely reasonable and well-grounded in facts, stirred up such a storm of outrage that Summers soon received a vote of no confidence by the faculty and was eventually forced to resign from his role as President.

---

[17] Marcella Bombardieri, "Summers' Remarks on Women Draw Fire," *Boston Globe* (January 17, 2005), accessed April 26, 2018, http://archive.boston.com/news/ education/higher/articles/2005/01/17/summers_remarks_on _women_draw_fire/.

One of the core beliefs of academics in elite American higher education is that men and women are equal. This sounds very noble, but it is interpreted to mean that aside from anatomical differences, men and women are the same. This belief is so strongly held that it rises to the level of religion and cannot be questioned. For adherents to this faith, there can only be one acceptable answer as to why there are fewer women in traditionally male dominated fields such as math and science. That answer is sexism.

The remedy for this grave sin is re-education. Universities devote entire departments to studying these alleged crimes, and then funnel their discoveries into the classroom. Male students are invited to grieve for the historical subjugation of women by men, and then attend diversity trainings to rid themselves of bias. These trainings may not end upon graduation, but may continue under the diversity and inclusion programs of their future employer. Those in higher education have successfully proselytized an entire generation of American elite.

The belief in literal gender equality is also broadcasted to the public at large through popular culture. In the blockbuster film *Star Wars: The Last Jedi*, the protagonist is a young woman who is able to defeat elite male soldiers in hand-to-hand combat. The movie also features a cast of female com-

manders taking on an entirely male (and evil) enemy fleet. The movie challenges one of the core differences between men and women: physical
strength. It also challenges the assumption of the
military being a male dominated institution, which
it has always been. A fundamental assumption the
movie makes is that women can do everything men
can.

These portrayals are sharply at odds with reality
and would have been ridiculous to audiences only a
few decades ago. Men have significantly more upper body strength than women, such that even a
teenage boy can easily overpower a grown woman.
There's no way a girl can defeat a grown man in
hand-to-hand combat. By extension, men are much
better at fighting than women, so it should not be
surprising that the military is overwhelmingly men
at all levels. Despite these obvious facts, belief in
literal gender equality has funneled through much
of American society. Indeed, the U.S. has recently
allowed women to join military combat roles. Like
many other religious beliefs, belief in literal gender
quality is immune to facts.

Men are from Mars, Women are from Venus was
one of the bestselling books in the 1990s. In his
book, Dr. Gray noted that there are fundamental
differences in the psychology of men and women.
Broadly speaking, men value power, competency,

efficiency, and achievement while women value love, communication, beauty, and relationships. These differences often lead to misunderstandings. In a classic example, a woman complaining about her job is looking for empathy and emotional validation. But when a man hears the complaint, he understands it as a problem to be solved and so offers a solution. He says, "How about you find another job?" This provides a logical solution but misses the point of the complaint, which is a request for emotional support.

Dr. Gray's book, which provided valuable insight for millions of people, would not be welcomed today. It would be labelled as sexist, a grave offense that merits outright dismissal. Yet it is intuitively obvious to all people that there are some differences between how men and women think. These differences may be biologically based and beyond the influence of even the most intensive diversity training. Despite the wholesale taboo of the exploration of these topics in many fields, evolutionary psychologists have made significant discoveries on the fundamental psychological differences between the sexes.

The sections below sketch out some major differences between men and women with respect to their social organization, personality traits, dating preferences, and intelligence. These differences will show that men are born to be the builders and defenders of civilization, while women are born to be mothers.

Social Organization

Even at an early age, boys and girls behave differently when they're in same-sex groups.[18] Boys tend to form large hierarchal groups oriented around common activities. Within same-sex groups, boys will openly compete with each other, interrupt each other often, heckle each other, or boast. But a group of boys is able to quickly put their differences aside and unite to achieve common goals. Think of a group of men on a sports team, casually trash talking each other but still working together as a team. Girls tend to form smaller intimate groups of two or three. Within same sex groups, girls share secrets, take turns when speaking, and are more inclined to express agreement with one another. Think of how girls behaved in school; they were often gossiping and laughing with their best friend.

Across cultures, the discussions women have with each other center around their relationships and personal problems.[19] Women discuss problems they

---

[18] Eleanor Maccoby, "Gender and Relationships, A Developmental Account," *American Psychologist* 45, no. 4 (April 1990), 513-520.
[19] Joyce F. Benenson and Athena Christakos, "The Greater Fragility of Females' Versus Males' Closest Same-Sex

have with other women, problems with their romantic partners, and their fears. In contrast, men often discuss activities or common interests, but are less inclined to talk about their personal problems.[20]

The larger, hierarchal groups that men form tend to center around activities with specific goals, such as defeating the other team, increasing profit, or fighting wars. The smaller groups that women form tend to be deeper relationships that can be an important source of emotional support. Indeed, across cultures one of the key differences between men and women is the higher reliance by women on other members of the same-sex for emotional support. [21] Within their same-sex networks, women tend to be more open to sharing changes in status such as illness, offering support, and receiving support. Men tend to not rely on their same-sex members for emotional support.

Since men and women build relationships for different reasons, they also judge their potential

Friendships," *Child Development* 74, no. 4 (July 2003), 1123-1129.
[20] Mayta Caldwell and Letitia Peplau, "Sex Differences in Same-Sex Friendship," *Sex Roles* 8, no. 7 (July 1982), 721-732.
[21] Shelley E. Taylor et al. "Behavioral Responses to Stress in Females: Tend-and-Befriend, Not Fight-or-Flight," *Psychological Review* 107, no. 3 (July 2000), 411-429.

friends by different criteria. Joyce Benenson, a leading researcher on gender differences, saw this manifest at an early age through a series of interviews with elementary school children. She noted boys judged other boys by their respective expertise, where one boy would be judged by his peers to be good at academics, another in his athletic ability, etc. [22] In contrast, girls only judged other girls by how nice they were. Consistent with how boys and girls organized themselves socially, boys valued other boys who would be strong team members while girls valued other girls who might be willing to provide personal support.

Competitive team sports are a good illustration of the quintessential male group type. On a sports team, members specialize in different roles and work together to defeat another team. Across cultures, men display at least twice as much interest in competitive sports than women. This is even true in the U.S., where laws require a school to devote substantial resources to female sports activities. These requirements have significantly raised female participation in school sports, but that doesn't mean that women are as interested in team sports as men are. On average, men report spending more time than women playing team sports, and men are ob-

---

[22] Joyce Benenson, "Gender Differences in Social Networks," *Journal of Early Adolescence* 10, no. 4 (November 1, 1990), 472-495.

served playing team sports in public parks at significantly higher rates than women. Furthermore, women who are involved in sports tend to participate in non-team sports like running and swimming. [23]

One other very important difference in how men and women organize themselves is in the importance of rules. This difference can again be seen at an early age. Boys, being competitive and group oriented, tend to engage in activities that have elaborate rules such as baseball or soccer. [24] The rules are followed closely by the participants and form a framework to manage the large number of participants and resolve conflict. Girls tend to not play games with elaborate rules. In the event of conflict in their games, girls simply terminate the game rather than argue over the rules as boys would. It is more important to a girl to maintain a relationship than be correct under the rules.

The emphasis on rules by men reflects a fundamental difference between how men and women decide what's right or wrong. A man would tend to consider an action wrong if it violates rules or principles

[23] Robert O. Deaner et al., "A Sex Difference in the Predisposition for Physical Competition: Males Play Sports Much More Than Females Even in the Contemporary U.S.," *PLoS One*, 7, no. 11 (November 14, 2012), e49168
[24] Janet Lever, "Sex Differences in the Games Children Play," *Social Problems* 23, no. 4 (April 1976), 478-487.

that he agrees to, but a woman would tend to consider an action wrong if it hurts someone else.[25] For example, men are much more likely than women to think that illegal immigrants who arrived in the U.S. when they were children should be deported.[26] Men place more value on the rule of law, but women are more sympathetic to the unfortunate plight of the illegal immigrants.

All our traditional institutions were built by men and correspondingly bear the marks of male forms of social organization. Religions, governments, and the military are large, hierarchal organizations governed by elaborate sets of rules intended to balance the interests of the members with those of the greater group. Conflicts between members within those respective organizations are resolved by reference to said set of rules. This type of organization is alien to female nature, which is more comfortable with smaller and more personal groups like families.

---

[25] Carol Gilligan, "In a Different Voice: Women's Conceptions of Self and of Morality," *Harvard Educational Review* 47, no. 4 (December 1977), 481-517.

[26] When asked how illegal immigrants who arrived in the U.S. as children should be treated, 19% of men polled believed they should be deported versus 8% of the women polled. The same poll showed that 45% of men polled supported a border wall with Mexico, compared to 37% of women polled. Quinnipac University Poll dated January 11, 2018.

It's no surprise that women have literally never built any large organization in all of history.

Social Behavior By Sex	
Men	**Women**
Prefer larger groups	Prefer smaller groups of 2
Activity based: sports, wars	Intimate: share secrets, feelings
More important to be correct. Strong emphasis on compliance with group determined rules	More important to maintain relationships than follow rules
Judge other men by expertise	Judge other women by how nice they are
Hierarchal	Egalitarian

Personality

In the old English epic poem *Beowulf,* the great warrior Beowulf confronts and defeats a menacing dragon that is terrorizing his people. In the Old Testament, King David was hailed as a hero for standing up against and defeating the giant Goliath. In modern times, movie heroes like Batman and Spiderman battle villains in defense of their cities. These heroes possess aggression, courage, and strength, and they exercise it in the context of protecting their people. They are heroes who exemplify masculine personality traits.

Across cultures and time, to be a man was to be a warrior. Groups of men have always been in constant warfare with each other. This happened in small village settlements, in city-states, in kingdoms, and in empires. In the great World Wars of the 20th century, tens of millions of men perished. The advanced industrialized world has enjoyed a period of peace in recent decades, but that's not the norm over the course of history.

Men fight not for themselves or even necessarily for their family, but for their tribe. The typical soldier in war has been young men who often don't have a wife or children, yet they go and put their life in harm's way. It has always been the role of men to work with other men and look after the interests of their tribe. As men fight for the survival of the group, women stay home and ensure the survival of their children. The focus of women through history has been the immediate and personal, which is also very important but does not require the same masculine traits.

Across cultures and time, to be a woman was to be a mother. While the typical modern family has two or fewer children, women historically typically had several children. This meant a lot of work to do and children to carefully monitor, particularly when child mortality has historically been extremely high. Traits that are traditionally considered feminine, such as gentleness, kindness, or nurturance, are also descriptions of good mothers.

The different circumstances confronting men and women over history has played a part in shaping the behavioral natures of the sexes. Masculine and feminine personality traits are not purely social constructs, but also hard coded in our biology. Cross-cultural studies have even shown that the more developed and gender equal a nation becomes, the larger the aggregate personality differences between men and women.[27] When there are fewer cultural constraints, men and women have greater freedom to behave according to their nature. Men on average are more violent, competitive, risk loving, interested in inanimate objects, and systemic in their thinking. Women on average are more empathetic, risk averse, and interested in people. The table below summarizes these differences and the following subsections below will go into more detail on each of these differences.

---

[27] Schmitt et al., "Can't a Man Be More Like a Woman? Sex Differences in Big Five Personality Traits Across 55 Cultures," *Journal of Personality and Social Psychology* 94, no. 1 (January 2008), 168-182.

Joseph King

Personality by Sex	
Men	**Women**
Thrives on competition	Avoids competition and conflict
More physically aggressive	Less physically aggressive
Lower anxiety and fearfulness	Higher anxiety, fearfulness, and depression
More open to risk taking	Less open to risk taking
More interested in ideas and inanimate things	More interested in people and relationships
Lower in nurturing qualities	Higher in nurturing qualities

Violence

When I was boy, my favorite toys were He-Man and GI-Joe figures. I would have them fight each other in countless scenarios. When I was a little older, my favorite toys were water guns. I would get together with the other boys in the neighborhood and we would have epic battles on the playground, complete with water balloon grenades. Even in college, my favorite pastime was getting together with other guys and playing video games in which we would try to kill each other with a wide variety of weapons.

It might be that I happened to be a particularly violent person, but this strong interest in fighting is observed in boys at an early age and across multiple cultures. The best-selling toys for boys always include weapons, and almost all the best-selling video games are about fighting enemies. This is true across the world from the U.S. to Europe to China. Archaeologists have even discovered toy soldiers and toy weapons in Egyptian ruins dating back thousands of years ago. The inescapable conclusion is that boys are born with an interest in fighting.

This would be consistent with the constant warfare between groups of men seen throughout history. In a world where war is common, men with an interest in fighting have a survival advantage. A brief look through history will show that war is a deadly business in which the losers can lose everything. When city of Carthage finally succumbed to siege by the Romans in 146 B.C., the Romans leveled the entire city and either killed or enslaved the entire population.[28] The Romans then went about and demolished all the smaller towns and cities that had supported Carthage. Throughout history, men who were good at fighting would have a better chance of surviving and passing on their fighter genes. Men who weren't good at fighting were killed, along with their families.

---

[28] Appian, *The Punic Wars*.

This interest in fighting can also be seen in measures of physical aggression. Research shows that across cultures, men are consistently more physically aggressive than women are.[29] Higher levels of aggression can even be seen even in infant males as young as 2 years old, so it's likely a genetic and not a socialized trait. Unsurprisingly, the murder rate of men is 10 times higher than the murder rate of women, with most victims also being men. It seems even in times of peace, men have an urge to fight other men, as they've done throughout history.

Murder Offenders and Victims by Sex in 2016

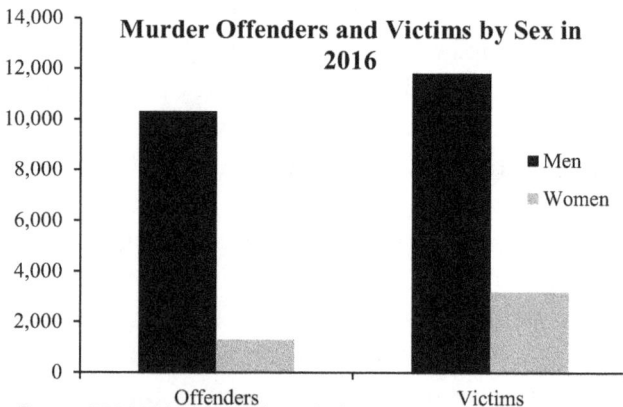

Source: FBI 2016 Crime in the United States, Expanded Homicide Data Tables 1, 2. Note: Chart does not include 5,359 unidentified murder offenders.

[29] John Archer, "Sex Differences in Aggression in Real-World Settings: A Meta-Analytic Review," *Review of General Psychology* 8, no. 4 (2004), 291-322.

In contrast to boys, girls exhibit no interest in fighting. The best-selling toys for girls are dolls and related doll apparel and accessories, which even include miniature houses where dolls can socialize with other dolls. None of the additional accessories are weapons, and none of the dolls are intended to fight each other. Girls take these dolls and have conversations with them as if they were people; in effect, they are pretending to be mothers. Girls can be seen playing with dolls across the world today and even as far back as in ancient Egypt. In fact, even juvenile female chimpanzees cradle sticks as if they were infants.[30] In the hands of a boy, a doll would be shooting fireballs out of its eyes against evil villains. Fighting cannot be a winning survival strategy for women because their relatively weak physical strength means they will virtually always lose to a male aggressor. But violence can help a man and his tribe survive.

Competition
Men like to compete. Even as far back as ancient Greece, men created the Olympics where athletes from each city-state could gather and compete. In any school across the world, teams of young men can be seen outside playing competitive sports like

---

[30] Sonya M. Kahlenberg and Richard W. Wrangham. "Sex Differences in Chimpanzees' Use of Sticks as Play Objects Resemble Those of Children," *Current Biology* 20, no. 24 (December 2010), R1067-R1068.

soccer or basketball. Men who aren't playing sports still enjoy watching them and can be seen enthusiastically congregating at sports bars when popular games are shown. Women are noticeably absent from any of these activities. Men openly compete against other men in all areas of their life, including professional success, academic achievement, and over women. Researchers have supported this every day observation with tests that show men to be significantly more open to competition than women.[31] For men, competition reveals competence and offers them an opportunity to rise in the male hierarchy.

Instead of competing openly, women make an effort to present themselves as equal to other women. Competition creates hierarchy and conflict, both of which are disagreeable to women. When members of an all-women group compete with each other, the winning woman feels uncomfortable and consistently downplays her success, attributing it to luck or hard work or some external factor.[32] But a winning man in a comparable circumstance tends to openly gloat and attribute his success to his su-

---

[31] Muriel Niederle and Lise Vesterlund, "Do Women Shy Away From Competition? Do Men Compete Too Much?" *The Quarterly Journal of Economics* 122, no. 3 (August 1, 2007), 1067–1101.

[32] Joyce Benenson, *Warriors and Worriers* (New York: Oxford University Press, 2014).

perior skill. For a woman, success may damage her relationships with other women, as it challenges the shared belief in equality held by her peer group.

While averse to open competition, women are competitive in more subtle ways.[33] A woman competes primarily against other women over things like mates, social status, and opportunities for her children. When a woman spends hours dressing up for a date, she's trying to outshine other women for a man's attention. When she posts images on social media of her exotic vacations or fancy meals, she is signaling to men that she has higher status than other women. Men typically don't spend nearly as much time as women on self-grooming or social media, as a man's status among men is less dependent upon appearances.

Historically, human societies have all been stratified by gender in which men have generally held all the positions of power. It didn't make sense for a woman to compete against a man, or for a man to compete against a woman because they lived in different social worlds. A woman couldn't raise her status by competing based on skill, as men did. The most direct way for a woman to improve her life

---

[33] Tracy Vaillancourt, "Do Human Females Use Indirect Aggression as an Intrasexual Competition Strategy?" *Philosophical Transactions of the Royal Society* 368, no. 1631 (October 2013).

was by marrying a high-status man, which would give her access to more resources and improve the chances of survival for her children. This meant a woman had to effectively compete against other women, perhaps by improving her appearance. If women with the genetic propensity to improve their appearance had more surviving children than women who were relative slobs, then it should be expected that, over time, that genetic propensity would become more common in the population. It may not be a coincidence that women throughout the world tend to have more extensive wardrobes and cosmetic collections than their male counterparts.

A woman's tools of competition are indirect: reputational slander and social exclusion. An aggrieved woman spreads rumors about or seeks to socially isolate an offending woman. She would do all this, and still smile politely as she passes her target on the street. Indirect competition allows a woman to remain anonymous and thus reduces the risk of retaliation. Only in rare, extreme, occurrences would a woman resort to physical force against another woman. In contrast, it's common for a man to openly confront or even physically challenge an offending man. Founding Father Alexander Hamilton was killed by Aaron Burr, the third Vice President of the United States, in a duel in 1804 over offensive remarks Hamilton had allegedly made.

Men like things; Women like people

On average, women express more interest in people while men express more interest in things.[34] This can be clearly seen in the subjects men and women in the United States choose to study in college, shown in the chart below. Fields like education, psychology, and health professions (including nursing) are dominated by women. For example, Columbia University's School of Social Work is around 85% women, which is typical for social work programs. On the other hand, men dominate fields such as engineering and computers where there is little interaction with people but more interaction with things. A cursory glance in any technical school or field would confirm this. A similar occupational gender gap is seen across countries in the European Union.[35] This suggests that the occupational gap is rooted in biology rather than socialization.

---

34 Rong Su, James Rounds, and Patrick Ian Armstrong, "Men and Things, Women and People: A Meta-Analysis of Sex Differences in Interests," *Psychological Bulletin* 135, no. 6 (November 2009), 859-884.
35 B. Burchell et al., "A New Method to Understand Occupational Gender Segregation in European Labour Markets," European Commission, Directorate-General for Justice (January 2014).

(1,000s)

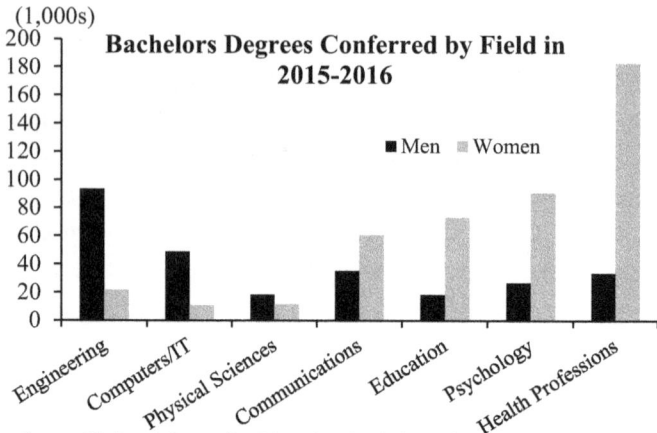

Bachelors Degrees Conferred by Field in 2015-2016

Source:National Center for Education Statistics, Digest of Education Statistics, Table 318.30

In fact, there is evidence that the more gender equal a country is the more striking the occupational gender gap is. Two researchers in Norway have made efforts to tackle this paradox by surveying boys and girls in forty countries on their attitudes towards science and technology.[36] The researchers found that across all countries boys have more interest in science and technology than girls have. When thinking about a future job, boys like working with their hands, things, machines, and tools while girls like working with and helping people.

[36] S. Sjøberg and C. Schreiner, "The ROSE Project: An Overview and Key Findings," University of Oslo (March, 2010), accessed April 26, 2018, http://roseproject.no/network/countries/norway/eng/nor-Sjoberg-Schreiner-overview-2010.pdf

The most interesting aspect of their study is that it finds the occupational gender gap to be wider among wealthier and more gender egalitarian countries than developing countries. One interpretation of this is that in poorer countries men and women are happy to take whatever job they can get, whereas in wealthier countries each sex has more financial freedom to pursue their interests.

The different interests men and women have should not be surprising in light of the different roles each sex has played throughout our evolutionary history. The primary role of women has been to take care of children, so it makes sense for them to have evolved a stronger interest in people. Women who genuinely like to care for other people would more likely have surviving offspring. Overtime, that means a growing proportion of women would have genes that promote interest in people.

The primary role of men has been to take care of their tribe. Men have been able to do this through understanding and manipulating the inanimate world, which has led to spears, castles, cars, and, ultimately, the advanced industrialized world we know today. Tribes of men with stronger interests in inanimate objects likely had better technology and were, thus, more likely to prevail in warfare and survive to pass on their genes. The classic example of this can be seen in how swiftly the British took over large parts of Africa in the 19th Century. Armed with superior technology, such as the Maxim gun (the first machine gun), a few hundred British could annihilate thousands of Africans. As put by British poet Belloc in his poem "The Modern Traveler," "Whatever happens, we have got the Maxim gun, and they have not."

Men take more risks; Women are more fearful

Across cultures, women report being more fearful and anxious than men.[37] In line with this, women are twice as likely to develop depression.[38] This heightened sense of anxiety is particularly salient when it comes to personal health. Despite having higher life expectancy than men have, women consistently report poorer health than men and have more frequent visits to the doctor.[39]

A review of 150 studies on risk taking showed that men are consistently more open to taking risks than women, particularly when it comes to physical

[37] C. P. McLean and E. R. Anderson, "Brave Men and Timid Women? A Review of Gender Differences in Fear and Anxiety," *Clinical Psychology Review*, 29 (2009)
[38] Susan Nolen-Hoeksema. Gender Differences in Depression. *Current Directions in Psychological Science*. (October 2011).
[39] K. D. Bertakis et al., "Gender Differences in the Utilization of Health Care Services," *Journal of Family Practice*, 49, no. 2 (February 2000), 147-152.

risks.[40] Men are more likely than women to drink heavily, use illicit drugs, drive unsafely, and use guns. [41] Similarly, race car drivers, coal miners, metal welders, and other highly dangerous occupations are virtually dominated by men. Men simply have less regard for their own physical safety. This can even be seen in the car insurance rates women pay, which are, on average, lower than what men pay because men have a higher accident rate.[42]

Historically, it pays for a man to take risks. A high status man not only has an easier time attracting a mate, but can also have multiple wives. The massive harems seen in some cultures suggest that at least some women prefer being the second, third, or even tenth wife of a highly successful man than the only wife of a low status man.[43] Because of this dynamic, many low status men may not be able to reproduce

---

[40] James P. Byrnes, David C. Miller, and William D. Schafer, "Gender Differences in Risk Taking: A Meta-Analysis," *Psychological Bulletin* 125, no 3 (1999).

[41] Ingrid Waldron. Gender and Health-Related Behavior, in *Health Behavior,* ed. D. S. Gochman (New York: Plenum, 1988), 193-208.

[42] National Association of Insurance Commissioners. *A Consumer's Guide to Auto Insurance* (2011).

[43] Many contemporary writers on gender dynamics in the U.S. have also noticed that women prefer the casual attention of a high status man over the full devotion of a low status man. *See* Rollo Tomassi, *The Rational Male* (2013).

at all. If a man takes risks, he might be able to improve his position and attract a mate.

On the other hand, risk taking doesn't improve a woman's chances of reproductive success. It's relatively easy for a woman to find a willing mate; her challenge is successfully raising the child. A woman's reproductive chances are maximized if she stays alive by staying out of danger.[44] This is because the survival of an infant is more dependent on a caring mom than a caring dad. Even beyond nursing the child, a mother is much more willing to invest in the survival of her child than the child's father. According to the U.S. Census, 85% of single parent households in the U.S. are headed by single mothers.[45] Men are much more willing than women to abandon their children. If a woman takes risks, she might die and leave her children without any support. Thus, a risk-averse mom has a higher likelihood of having a surviving child.

The different incentive structure for risk taking facing men and women likely led men and women to develop different innate risk preferences.

---

[44] Anne Campbell, "Staying Alive: Evolution, Culture, and Women's Intrasexual Aggression," *Behavioral and Brain Sciences* 22, no. 2 (1999), 203-214.
[45] United States Census 2016. America's Families and Living Arrangements: 2016 Table C3.

Nurturing

Women are stereotypically considered as the more nurturing sex. Researchers have confirmed this stereotype through studies that show women scoring higher than men in personality traits such as sensitivity, compassion, empathy, and warmth.[46,47] The gap between the sexes was generally found to be fairly large. One groundbreaking study has shown this gap to exist across twenty-six cultures, thus strongly suggesting a biological rather than cultural cause.[48] The same study found the gap to be largest in the U.S. and Western Europe, which are both the most gender egalitarian regions in the world. One possibility for this is that as the genders become more socially equal, their biology-based differences become more obvious. This would be a similar dynamic to the wide occupational segregation seen in gender-egalitarian Scandinavian countries noted earlier.

---

[46] M. Guidice, T. Booth, and P. Irwing, "The Distance Between Mars and Venus: Measuring Global Sex Differences in Personality," *PLoS ONE* 7, no. 1 (2012), e29265.
[47] Yanna J. Weisberg, Colin G. DeYoung, and Jacob B. Hirsh, "Gender Differences in Personality Across the Ten Aspects of the Big Five," *Frontiers in Psychology* 2 (August 1, 2011), 178.
[48] P. T. Costa, A. Terracciano, and R. R. McCrae, "Gender Differences in Personality Traits Across Cultures: Robust and Surprising Findings," *Journal of Personality and Social Psychology* 81, no. 2 (August 2001), 322-331.

This sex difference likely has to do with way labor has been traditionally divided among the sexes. Women everywhere undertake the lion's share of childcare. To get a better sense of how this responsibility could have shaped the female nature, it helps to think back a little to the historical circumstances in which humans evolved.

The average household size throughout history was much larger than it is today. Back then, all work was manual labor, so children were viewed as a resource. People liked having large families because the more people a family had, the more workers there were to gather food or farm. For example, Founding Fathers Thomas Jefferson and Benjamin Franklin each had nine siblings.[49,50] The preference for larger families has waned over time, as children have become more of an economic liability than an asset. In 1850, the average number of children per family in the U.S. was 3.5. That number is only a little over 1 today.

Child mortality rates have historically been very high until recent decades. As recently as 1915, one out of ten infants born in the U.S. died within 1 year

[49] The Franklin Institute, accessed April 26, 2018, https://www.fi.edu/benjamin-franklin-faq.
[50] Lisa A. Francavilla, "Thomas Jefferson and His Family," *Encyclopedia Virginia* (September 28, 2015), accessed April 26, 2018, https://www.encyclopediavirginia.org/Jefferson_Thomas_and_His_Family.

of birth. That was already a significant improve
ment over the 20% infant mortality rates anthro
pologists estimate in more primitive hunter
gatherer peoples. [51] Even after surviving infancy
only around half of the children born in these prim
itive conditions would live to age 15. Many childre
succumbed to disease, which was particularl
threatening in a world without electricity, runnin
water, or modern medicine. There was also th
threat of any number of unpredictable extern
events such as famine and war.

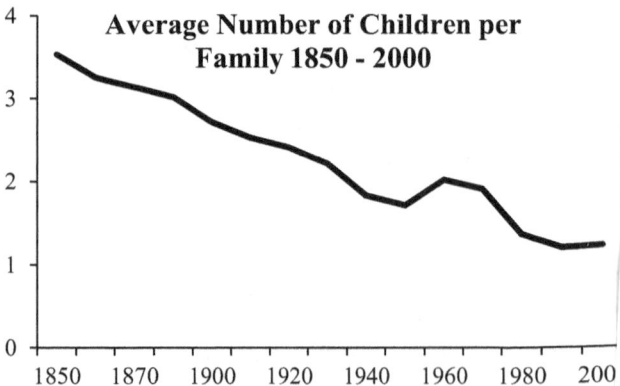

Average Number of Children per Family 1850 - 2000

Source:Salcedo, Schoellman,Tertile. Families as Roommates:
Changes in U.S. Household Size from 1850 to 2000.

---

[51] Michael Gurven and Hillard Kaplan, "Longevity
Among Hunter-Gatherers: A Cross-Cultural Examina
tion," *Population and Development Review* 33, no. ;
(June 2007) 321-365.

Infant Mortality Rate (deaths per 1000 infants)

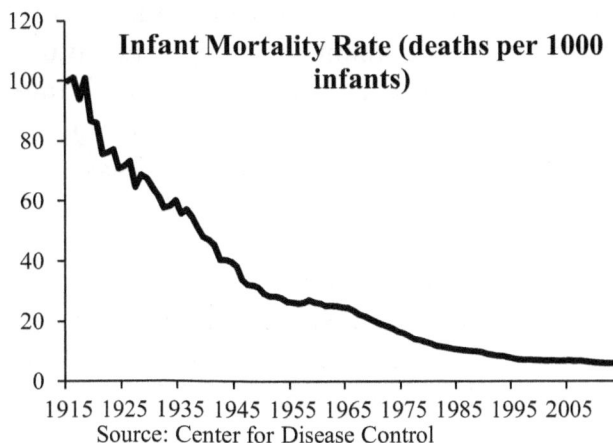

Source: Center for Disease Control

A large household size combined with high child-hood mortality rate implies that most women throughout history were pregnant a good part of their reproductive lives. Being a mom really was the primary job of most women throughout history. Given how difficult it was to raise children in the pre-modern world, a good mom would have literal-ly made the difference between life and death for her children. A good mom would be empathetic and sensitive to the needs of her children. In a word, she would be nurturing. Because nurturing moms would be more successful at having surviving off-spring, the genes that led to nurturing moms be-came more prevalent in our gene pool such that, on average, women became more nurturing than men.

Dating

Men and women value different things when it comes to dating, and the magnitude of the differences is large.[52] Some aspects of mate choice are cultural, but other aspects are biologically determined. This is a complicated topic, but the best way to distinguish between aspects that are cultural and those that are biologically hardwired is to look for aspects of mate choice that are true universally across cultures.

For example, Asian cultures tend to consider pale skin attractive for a woman while those in the West tend to prefer tan skin. Any department store in Asia will have a wide selection of skin-whitening creams advertised by pale, porcelain-skinned models. These skin-whitening products are nowhere to be found in the U.S., where, instead, many people spend money on tanning salons or suntan lotion. Skin tone preferences do not just vary by location, but also across time. Pre-modern Europe also shared the Asian preference for pale skin, which served as a status symbol to show that one was wealthy enough to not have to work in the fields under the sun. Since preference for skin tone varies significantly across the world and through time, it

---

[52] Daniel Conroy-Beam et al., "How Sexually Dimorphic Are Human Mate Preferences?" *Personality and Social Psychology Bulletin* 41, no. 8 (June 11, 2015), 1082-1093.

is likely a preference that is predominately culturally determined.

On the other hand, some preferences are universal across all cultures. For example, men across all cultures, from lawyers in the glass towers of New York City to Peruvian tribesmen, prefer women with hourglass figures. [53] Hourglass figures have been reliably linked to youth and health. Women universally prefer older, while men prefer younger women.[54] Given that these preferences are true across cultures, they're likely to be genetically based.

Men and women look for different things in mates because throughout history they've faced different reproductive problems. Before the introduction of public welfare, the survival of a woman and her children was highly dependent upon how good a provider her husband was. During pregnancy and in the child's infancy, a woman is limited in the work she can do and is especially physically vulner-

---

[53] Decendra Singh, "Female Mate Value at a Glance: Relationship of Waist-to-Hip Ratio to Health, Fecundity and Attractiveness," *Neuroendocrinology Letters* 23, suppl 4 (December 2002), 81-91.
[54] D. Buss, "Sex Differences in Human Mate Preferences: Evolutionary Hypotheses Tested in 37 Cultures," *Behavioral and Brain Sciences* 12 (1989), 1-49, accessed April 26, 2018, https://www.cambridge.org/core/ sevices/ aop-cambridge-core/content/view/ S0140525X00023992.

able. Raising children takes a lot of time and re-sources. Given these challenges, women who secure a good provider are more likely to be reproductively successful.

Across cultures, it appears that women consistently value traits that suggest a man may be a good pro-vider, such as ambition and industriousness. [55] Women's universal preference for older men is also likely to be because, on average, older men have more resources. Other elements highly correlated with wealth, such as a man's status, are also strong-ly emphasized by women. There's also a lot of evi-dence that women prefer physical traits in mates that suggest an ability to provide physical security, such as height.[56]

Men have been faced with an entirely different problem when it comes to reproduction. For a man to be reproductively successful he has to find wom-en who are healthy and fertile. Men can reproduce well into old age, but a woman's fertility peaks in her early 20s. There is also a relationship between a woman's physical beauty and health, where beauty

---

[55] *Ibid.*
[56] Abigail Weitzman and Dalton Conley, "From Assorta-tive to Ashortative Coupling: Men's Height, Height Het-erogamy, and Relationship Dynamics in the United States," NBER (August 2014), accessed April 26, 2018, http://www.nber.org/papers/w20402.pdf.

is a sign of good health.[57] Across cultures, men consistently express a preference for younger and physically attractive women. They also generally prefer women with feminine personality traits.

Men are also more promiscuous than women across cultures.[58] Men have an innate desire for variety that is largely absent from women. Whereas a man would rarely pass-up an opportunity to have sex, a woman is more selective with her mates.[59] A promiscuous man would likely have more surviving offspring simply because he has more children. A promiscuous woman will likely become a single mom, which in the days before the welfare state meant poverty and social ostracism. This meant there was a good chance her child wouldn't survive. Sexual promiscuity is an evolutionary dead-end for a woman.

None of these findings should be surprising. In everyday life, we see men fawn over young and attractive twenty something women even when the men are old enough to be grandparents. Billionaires and

[57] J. Weeden and J. Sabini, "Physical Attractiveness and Health in Western Societies: A Review," *Psychological Bulletin* 131, no. 5 (September 2005), 635-653.

[58] Donald Symons. *The Evolution of Human Sexuality* (New York, Oxford University Press, 1971).

[59] Russell Clark and Elaine Hatfield, "Gender Differences in Receptivity to Sexual Offers," *Journal of Psychology & Human Sexuality* 2, no. 1 (1989), 39-55.

other high-status men routinely date and marry women young enough to be their daughters. For example, billionaire President Donald Trump's wife Melania is over 20 years younger than Mr. Trump. She is also his third wife. Billionaire Secretary of Treasury Steve Mnuchin's wife is around 20 years younger than he is. Both women are very attractive, Mrs.Trump being a former model and Mrs.Mnuchin a former actress.

None of this not to say that women do not value a man's looks – they do, but not nearly as much as a man value's a woman's looks. Women tend to express admiration for older, well-established men despite them being less physically attractive than younger men. Quite a few women would be willing to date or even marry a wealthy but ugly older man. It is much, much rarer for a man to marry a very wealthy but older woman. Men appear to value beauty and youth in a woman above all else.

One other important difference worth noting is that men and women are on different biological clocks when it comes to reproduction. Women are most fertile from their late-teens to early-thirties, after which it becomes increasingly difficult for a woman to conceive. Men have are able to conceive throughout their life, though younger men have higher quality sperm. For women who are interested in having children, this necessarily implies some degree of life planning that is different from how a man would plan his life. A man can work hard and build a career before deciding to have a family in his 30s, but a woman who chooses that same path is sacrificing her best childbearing years and may have trouble having a healthy child.

Dating by Sex	
Men	**Women**
Prefer a woman who is younger	Prefer a man who is older
High emphasis on physical attractiveness	Value wealth, status and height
Prefer nurturing, gentleness and other traits linked to good mothers	Prefer ambitious, industrious men
Sexually promiscuous	Sexually selective

Intelligence
In every profession, there are many successful women, but very few great women. This reflects a difference in how intelligence is distributed in men and women. Intelligence tests like IQ have a bell curve distribution for both sexes, but for most tests, the tails for the male distribution are fatter.[60] This

---

[60] L. Hedges and A. Nowell, "Sex Differences in Mental Test Scores, Variability, and Numbers of High-Scoring Individuals," *Science* 269, no. 5220 (July 1995) 41-45.

means males have more variability in their intelligence. So, in any population, most of the geniuses would be men, but also most of the dumbest people. In contrast, test scores of women tend to be more clustered around the average. This implies that the most eminent people of any field are going to be mostly men.

This is exactly what we see when we look through history. With respect to science and engineering, titans like Newton and Einstein stand out, but the list of brilliant scientists and engineers is very long. In the past century mankind's accomplishments include splitting the atom, putting a man on the moon, and building an internet that allows a person to access all the information ever known from anywhere in the world. Thousands of people worked hard and built on each other's work to accomplish these feats. One thing they have in common is that they are almost all men.

The same pattern can be seen in other fields such as the fine arts. The greatest composers in history (Beethoven, Mozart, and Bach to name a few) are virtually all men. The same pattern is also apparent in art, film, and literature. Van Gogh, Picasso, Monet, Da Vinci, Shakespeare, Dickens, Tolstoy etc. were all men. The pattern is clear: the most extraordinary among us are almost all men. Of course, there have been extraordinary women as well, but not very many. Even in today's gender-egalitarian world, almost all the most eminent people in every field continue to be predominately men. This is what we would expect based on the IQ distributions.

While IQ is used to measure a sort of "general" intelligence, there are also particular aspects of intelligence that on average differ between men and women. [61] Studies have consistently shown that women are more emotionally attuned to the feelings of other people, while men are better at systemizing. Systemizing means looking at a set of facts and deducing the logical relationships between them. A woman's mind is built to understand people, while a man's mind is built to understand inanimate things. This is in line with men's greater interest in "things" and women's greater interest in people. It's hard to quantitatively evaluate one's empathetic skills, but a person's systemizing ability can be tested using math tests.

On average, men have consistently scored above women on the math section of the Scholastic Aptitude Test ("SAT"). While the score gap has slightly narrowed since the 1970s, it has remained about 30 points in recent decades. However, the difference in

---

[61] Simon Baron-Cohen, "The Extreme Male Brain Theory of Autism," *TRENDS in Cognitive Sciences* 6, no. 6 (June 2002), 248-254, accessed April 26, 2018, http://cogsci.bme.hu/~ivady/bscs/read/bc.pdf.

average score hides large differences on the high end of the score distribution.

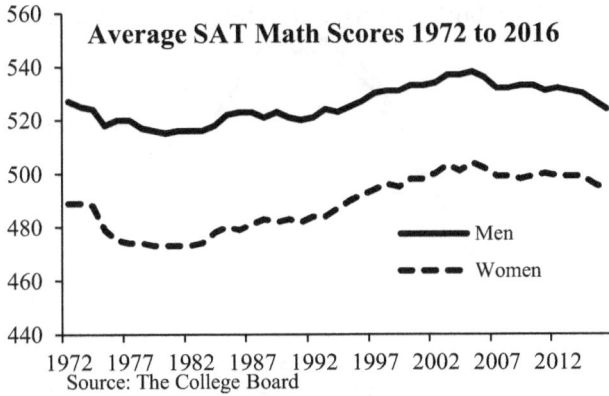

Average SAT Math Scores 1972 to 2016

—— Men

- - - Women

Source: The College Board

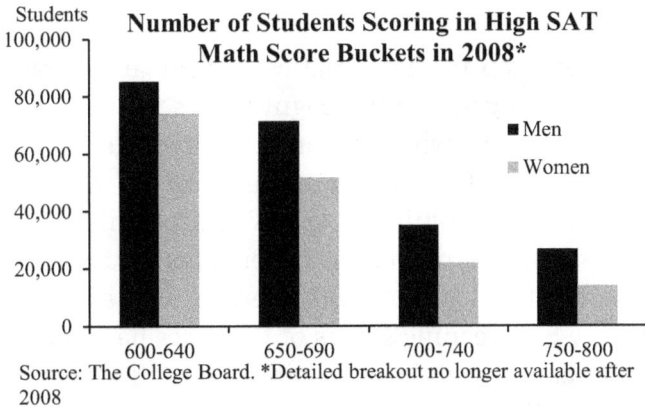

Number of Students Scoring in High SAT Math Score Buckets in 2008*

Students

■ Men

▨ Women

Source: The College Board. *Detailed breakout no longer available after 2008

Roughly twice as many men than women score above 750 (the maximum score is 800) on the test. This difference is reflected in the dominance of men in technical fields such as engineering and technology we see in everyday life.

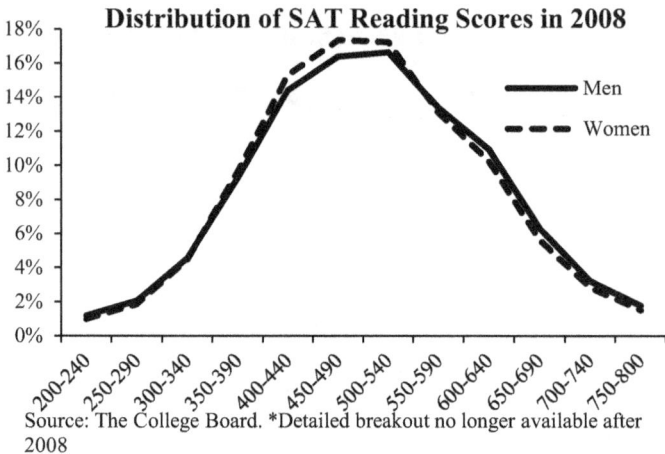

Distribution of SAT Reading Scores in 2008

Source: The College Board. *Detailed breakout no longer available after 2008

The score gap in mathematics is clear and persistent, but the gap in other cognitive tests tends to be relatively small when it comes to average scores. However, the distribution of men's scores on other cognitive tests continues to have fatter tails, while the distribution of women's scores continues to be more clustered around the average. For example, average SAT reading scores of the sexes have a negligible gap of only a few points, but 1.8% of men scored in the highest 750-800 bucket, and a slightly lower 1.5% of women scored in that bucket. This means that although the average man and woman have roughly the same score, a much higher number of men than women scored in the top bucket.

The systemizing mind has been responsible for virtually all of civilization. A few thousand years ago, we were living in mud huts and running around barefooted looking for animals to eat. There was no internet, no lights, no running water, and medicine meant appeasing the gods. The quality of life we have today would be unimaginable to even a person living just 100 years ago. All this is due to advances in man's ability to understand and manipulate the inanimate universe through science and technology.

While benefits of a systemizing mind are clear, it's less clear why men developed it. One possibility is that having a systemizing mind would have likely been helpful in many endeavors that have been traditionally within the realm of men. This would include the fields of commerce, engineering, science, or warfare. As noted earlier, groups of men good at systemizing would likely have better technology and survive in inter-group warfare. But even within a group, a man good at systemized thinking would likely be more successful in any traditionally male field. This would raise his status within the male community, which would increase his resources and attractiveness to women. This would have conferred reproductive advantages to men good at systemized thinking, which, over time, would increase the prevalence of genes that promote systemized thinking in the population.

Joseph King

Feminization of Society

On January 21ˢᵗ, 2017, just a day after the inauguration of President Trump, half a million people marched through Washington D.C. in a protest called the Women's March. Millions of others engaged in similar protests in cities across the country, with some experts even claiming that it was the largest one-day protest in the history of the United States.[62] According to the march's organizers, the Women's March stood for women's rights, LGBTQIA rights, worker's rights, civil rights, disability rights, immigrant rights, and environmental justice.[63] In other words, it stood for nothing. The protestors swapped stories, carried colorful signs, and then went home satisfied in their righteous indignation. No one seemed to be aware that the

---

[62] Matt Broomfield, "Women's March Against Donald Trump Is the Largest Day of Protests in US History, Say Political Scientists" *The Independent* (January 23, 2017).
[63] Women's March's Unity Principles, accessed April 26, 2018, https://www.womensmarch.com/mission

United States is one of the few countries in the history of the world that provides women with equal rights to men.

In many ways, the Women's March was a reflection of female psychology. It seemed that the fundamental purpose of the protest was not to achieve any objective goal, but to provide emotional support to the protestors in the wake of Mr. Trump's victory. The protest was egalitarian and inclusive of all grievance groups, to the point of having no real message. No one felt comfortable enough to stand up and assert leadership by establishing priorities and tangible goals; that would imply some people were more important than others. Disagreements within groups led to recriminations that were resolved through splintering.[64] It shouldn't be surprising to see that months later, nothing came of the protests. A Men's march would not have ended the same way.

Women and men are wired differently. If women and men were equal through and through, then one would think that somewhere in the annals of history there might be a great female built and led civilization, but no such thing exists. Women have never been the architects or builders of any civilization. It is not in their nature. This is not to say that women

[64] Carter Sherman, "The Women's March Isn't for Everyone," *Vice* (November 9, 2017).

are inferior, just that they are different. While men organize large groups of unrelated men into nations, women raise families and nurture our future generations.

Everything in the world is built and maintained by men. The roads the Women's March protestors walked on were built by men, their physical safety was maintained by a predominately male police force, and even the electricity that their microphones depended on was most likely supplied by men operating a power plant, which would also have been built and designed by men. If women went on strike for a day, there would be a lot of disruption and everything would slow down, but if men went on strike for a day there would rioting and looting in the streets.

Yet many in our country persist in adhering to a religion of literal equality. Their refusal to acknowledge fundamental differences between the sexes has enabled a gradual feminization of society by denying the existence of masculine viewpoints and concealing feminine viewpoints as neutral viewpoints. By forcing everyone to think of men and women as products of socialization rather than biology, feminine viewpoints gain equal legitimacy to masculine viewpoints. A culture that acknowledges the greater role men play in maintaining civilization would place greater emphasis on their viewpoints, but one that does not acknowledge this truth would not accord male viewpoints extra weight. Traditionally, men have been dismissive of the views of women on matters outside of the home. Now that our culture no longer acknowledges the greater importance of masculine viewpoints, feminine viewpoints have space to gain influence.

Since the feminist revolution, our culture has become increasingly feminized. The movement of women into the workforce, sometimes into positions of power, has given them opportunities to exert significant influence on our culture. Whereas in previous generations, women were primarily homemakers, women today earn more than half of all college degrees and can be seen in all professional fields. They bring their feminine viewpoints into the universities and workplace. In addition, an increasing percentage of children are being raised without a father. Together this implies a shift over the generations where the younger generation is increasingly feminized in their thinking. This is clearest when comparing prevailing viewpoints today to those prevailing historically, when men and their masculine viewpoints dominated all of culture. A few examples below illustrate this shift in the context of our culture's view of violence, meritocracy, confidence and truth.

No Violence

Scipio Africanus, a Roman general, led his army to a stunning victory against Rome's archenemy Carthage in 202 BC. On his return, he was showered with praise and honored with a grand parade, one of highest honors a Roman can receive. Scipio marched his army and prisoners through the streets of Rome, and paid for days of games and festivals out of his portion of the spoils of war.[65] The public was ecstatic at Rome's victory, and proud of the growing reach of their empire. People in that era didn't mind sending men out to slaughter foreigners and take their possessions. But military activities today, whether it be to fight communists in Vietnam or gain control over oil-rich countries in the Middle East, are met with stiff protest. Protestors protest the loss of life, the cruelty towards foreigners, and the illegitimacy of violence as a solution to conflict.

How does history go from a story of conquest to one where violence is bad? The answer is that the actors in the story have changed. As recently as 100 years ago, men were waging war against other men, defeating them, and then ruling over them. The way of men had been the way of gangs.[66] The British Empire at one point ruled over 20% of the world's

---

[65] Polybius. *Histories,* Book 16.
[66] Jack Donavan. *The Way of Men* (Dissonant Hum, 2012).

population and held vast amounts of land such that the sun never set on the Empire. The Nazi Third Reich ruled over all of Continental Europe and came close to taking over Russia. The Japanese Empire, not content with controlling China and Korea, was bold enough to mount an assault against the United States. War was a source of glory, but also part of life. Today, it is greeted with protests, especially by women.

Women don't like violence and aren't violent. From school fights to bar fights to violent crime, men are, by far, the most common perpetrators. Throughout history, men go to war with other men, and never the women. The growing influence of women in the modern world has made war and other solutions based on force increasingly unpopular and unfeasible. Feminists, in particular, can be counted on to aggressively protest any military engagement, as they have through vocal but silly groups such as CodePink and Femen. This has been very positive for world peace, in which advanced industrialized nations have avoided major wars for decades.

But the feminine anti-violence view goes further than being anti-war. Looking across our news media, it seems that there has been a shift in attitude against all agents of force. The police are cast as trigger-happy thugs, and our military is viewed as imperialistic forces picking on colored third-world countries. The death penalty and intense interrogation are also strongly condemned. It seems that a growing segment of people view all violence as inherently wrong, because our enemies and bad guys are people too. They have feelings and dreams just like us, so we shouldn't hurt them.

In 2014, a white police officer shot and killed a black teen named Michael Brown in Ferguson, Missouri. Brown, a six foot four inch three hundred pound teen, was filmed stealing from a convenience store and shoving the store clerk. After Brown left the store, he encountered the police officer, and the ensuing conflict left Brown dead of a gunshot wound. While the police officer claimed that he shot Brown as Brown charged him, others claimed that Brown was shot with his hands in the air, pleading for his life. Mass protests and riots flared up around the country claiming police brutality. The FBI and DOJ descended upon Ferguson and conducted their own extensive investigations, but their findings corroborated the police officer's account.[67] This was a classic case of a thug being shot by a police officer, but because the thug died, and he was a black teen, the officer was blamed. To the eyes of the feminized public, the officer was in the wrong because he used force against someone per-

---

[67] Adam Howard, "Department of Justice Report Corroborates Darren Wilson's Story," *MSNBC* (March 4, 2015).

ceived as a weaker member of society. But his use of force made his community safer by taking out a thug and sending a signal that crime is not tolerated.

The French hold a military parade each year to celebrate Bastille Day, the Fourth of July of France. President Trump was very impressed by the parade when he saw it in 2017 and decided to plan a similar parade in the U.S. to celebrate our nation and military.[68] Honoring our military and showcasing its strength has been a common act throughout history, after all, our safety depends on their strength. Feminists and other left wing groups predictably panned the idea as silly, wasteful, or terrifying.[69] Some viewed the parade as so threatening that they vowed to lie down before the tanks in the fashion of the Tiananmen protest in China.[70] It's difficult to believe that there would be this degree of protest to something so conventional in the days before the rise of feminism.

---

[68] Matt Stevens, "Trump's Military Parade Plans Come Into Focus: Planes, But No Tanks," *New York Times* (March 9, 2018).

[69] Fiona Landers, "Everyone Hates a Parade," *Dame Magazine* (February 9, 2018).

[70] Jon Levine, "Trump's Tiananmen Square? Protesters Vow to Lie Down in Front of Tanks at Military Parade," *The Wrap* (February 7, 2018).

Joseph King

The death penalty, a punishment as old as civilization itself, is on its way to extinction. In the past,
virtually all nations executed criminals publically in
part to remind the public of the penalty of crime.
The growing resistance to the death penalty likely
comes from the feminization of society, as research
has consistently found that women are significantly
less likely than men to support the death penalty.[71]
Instead of offering the death penalty, we now house
and feed criminals for decades and then release
them into society, where many of them relapse into
crime. Being softer in punishment may also have an
effect on the amount of crime in our country. For
example, Singapore has a mandatory death penalty
for drug traffickers and, consequently, virtually no
drug problem.[72]

Torturing our enemies has also become an increasingly controversial issue. After 9/11, President Bush
invaded Afghanistan in an effort to dismantle al-
Qaeda's terrorist network. In the ongoing conflict,
enemies perceived as high value were captured and
held in a secret prison located in Guantanamo Bay,

[71] John K. Cochran and Beth A. Sanders, "The Gender
Gap in Death Penalty Support: An Exploratory Study,"
Journal of Criminal Justice 37, no. 6 (December 2009),
525-533.
[72] Singapore Ministry of Home Affairs. "Keeping Singapore Drug-Free," accessed April 26, 2018,
https://www.gov.sg/microsites/budget2018/press-
room/news/content/keeping-singapore-drug-free

Cuba. A public uproar ensued when news of the facility found its way to the press. Throughout its use, Guantanamo Bay held around 800 prisoners, many of whom were subject to enhance interrogation techniques such as waterboarding. Some were also subject to abuse. The facility and the enhanced interrogation methods used were politically very contentious and a frequent topic of protest. [73]

When men ruled the world, torturing enemies for information was par for the course in war. The information they received from the interrogation could help their nation. As for the wellbeing of the enemy, that didn't matter because he was an enemy. The lives of their own people were more important than the wellbeing of the enemy. But today, our mainstream media publishes long personal stories about prisoners in Guantanamo Bay to humanize them.[74] They talk about the families of the prisoners and the posttraumatic stress the prisoners have experienced since leaving Guantanamo, but not about the American lives saved from the information extracted. It seems as if the violence suffered by the enemy combatants was the only thing that mattered.

---

[73] Ian Simpson, "Protesters mark Guantanamo Prison's 10th anniversary, *Reuters* (January 11, 2012).
[74] Matt Apuzo, Sheri Rink, and James Risen, "How U.S. Torture Left a Legacy of Damaged Minds," *New York Times* (October 9, 2016).

Joseph King

Some women even extend their aversion to violence to animals. The animal rights movement, which is dedicated to ending cruelty towards animals and compassion towards all living things, is a movement overwhelmingly comprised of women.[75] Activists within the movement are against a range of activities including animal testing and meat eating. These activities benefit humans by helping us develop safer drugs and keeping us well fed. However, animal rights activists view the use of force against animals as categorically wrong. It would be absurd to think that men, who have so frequently killed each other through history, would care about the feelings of animals. The rise of the animal rights movement coincides closely with the rise of feminism.

Violence has no place in a feminized society. This presents a problem because violence is a fundamental pillar of any nation. Violence is what keeps public order within a country and keeps foreign invaders out. At times, it can also enhance a nation by extending the nation's resources and interests through conquest. By denying the important role of violence, we undermine a foundation of our nation. The feminized society is one that despises the very

[75] Rachel Einwohner. Gender, Class, And Social Movement Outcomes, Identity and Effectiveness in Two Animal Rights Campaigns. *Gender & Society*, Vol. 13 No. 1, (February 1999) 56-76.

masculine principles that enable it. Women, with their belief in nonviolence, have never built any nation or community. This isn't to say that all violence is good, but violence has an important role in maintaining our nation that should be acknowledged and respected.

No Competition

One of the fundamental values women hold is equality. Women avoid competition and are uncomfortable with hierarchy, particularly when it implies that one woman is superior to another. In an egalitarian world, no one needs to feel bad about oneself because there are no winners or losers. In contrast, hierarchy is an idea that is natural to men. Since childhood, men work together in groups where lower status males defer to higher status males. Men judge each other by their place in the hierarchy, which is determined largely by competence. This is most clearly seen in the military, in which a strict chain of command determines status.

Women judge one another by how "nice" they are. That is to say, how inoffensive and cordial one is. Men like to compete with one another, and do so openly in various formal and informal competitions from the speed one chugs a beer to sporting tournaments. In the competitive process, men openly taunt one another, with the eventual victor gloating over the losers. Women are far less likely to engage in similar behavior; it simply isn't nice. But men constantly compete with each other to obtain higher status and rise in the male hierarchy.

The rise of feminism corresponds with a decline in competition, and an emphasis on feeling good about oneself. For example, in 2015, a high school in Virginia named 117 valedictorians out of a graduating class size of 457.[76] Similarly, a recent poll shows a clear generational shift on how participation trophies are viewed. Over 50% of younger people believe all kids should receive participation trophies while older generations feel only winning kids should receive a trophy.

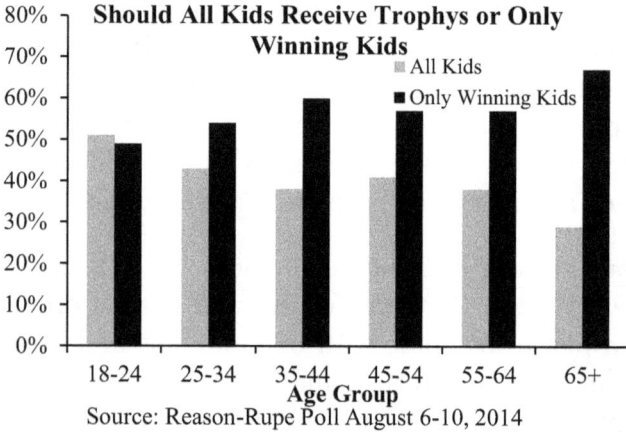

Should All Kids Receive Trophys or Only Winning Kids
All Kids
Only Winning Kids
Age Group
Source: Reason-Rupe Poll August 6-10, 2014

---

[76] Moriah Balingit, "The New Trend in Validating Top Students: Make Them All Valedictorians," *The Washington Post* (July 12, 2015).

This trend has negative implications not only for individuals but also on a national scale. While less competition can protect people from the disappointments of defeat, it doesn't help them improve. Without objective standards and feedback, people cannot have an honest view of themselves and figure out the areas where they need to grow. It's also very difficult to for them to build self-confidence without having triumphed over adversity and achieved real accomplishments.

Competition, and thus hierarchy, is essential to any well-run organization or country. If all employees are valued equally, regardless of merit, then there's limited incentive for good work. The best workers leave for companies that value talent and good work. Socialist countries like France have attempted to create equality by heavily taxing their most productive workers and redistributing the proceeds to others, but that just caused the most productive workers to move to lower taxed countries like the UK.[77] France was left with lower tax revenue and a less talented workforce.

In recent years, equality-based political views such as socialism have become increasingly prominent. Bernie Sanders, an avowed socialist, was a major

[77] Anne-Elisabeth Moutet, "Down and Out: The French Flee a Nation in Despair," *The Telegraph* (October 20, 2013).

contender in the 2016 presidential election. Polls also show younger Americans to hold favorable views of socialism.[78] Socialism, which emphasizes equality regardless of merit, appears to be the most appealing political system to a feminized generation.

The rise of feminism also coincides with the rise of affirmative action and other diversity and inclusion initiatives, where people are judged not by their abilities but by their identities. The goal of these initiatives is to have proportional representation across identity groups so no one feels left out. This trend completely undermines the competitive meritocratic principles that underlie any organization built by men. In the military, soldiers advance by proving themselves in their endeavors. On a sports team, players are given roles according to their abilities. In a traditional company, employees are promoted according to their contributions and competence. Judging a person by anything other than competence would be placing personal feelings above the goals of the organization. Men instinctively realize that as a poor way to manage a group.

The trend away from meritocracy has real implications. In March of 2018, a newly built bridge in Miami suddenly collapsed and crushed the cars driv-

---

[78] Max Ehrenfreund, "A Majority of Millennials Now Reject Capitalism, Poll Shows," *Washington Post* (April 26, 2016).

ing underneath. The sudden collapse of a bridge would be unremarkable news in many third world countries, but it's unheard of in the United States. A little digging revealed that the bridge was constructed by a minority-owned firm with a history of shoddy work.[79] The firm proudly champions its certified minority-owned status, which gives it a significant advantage when bidding for government contractors. If construction bidding for the bridge had been purely competence based, that bridge might not have collapsed.

In early 2018, the Federal Reserve Bank of New York launched a search for a successor to its retiring president. The president of the New York Fed is among the most influential people in the financial world because that office has direct input on monetary policy. After an exhaustive search, John Williams was nominated for the role. Williams was an eminent economist, president of the San Francisco Fed, and spent most of his career in public policy. Yet, many protested his nomination because he was a white man. New Jersey Senator Cory Booker, a black man who likely owed his career to identity politics, even penned a column openly campaigning

---

[79] James Kirkpatrick, "The Cost of Diversity: Florida Bridge Collapse Company a 'Certified Minority Owned Firm,'" *VDare* (March 16, 2018).

against any candidate that was a white man. [80] While the nomination this time was made on merit, it could have easily gone to a significantly less competent person based on skin color. Powerful interests were willing to risk the wellbeing of the global financial system simply so minorities could feel more included in policy choices.

The organizing principle for any group of men has always been merit. Each man competes with one another to find his place in the group. Competition encourages each person to improve himself, provides objective measures of success, and moves each person to the place best suited to his skills. This is an important part of the process of growing up. By shielding everyone from hurt feelings, feminists nurtured a generation of adults who are more fragile and less competent than those of earlier generations. By hiring people on criteria other than competence, our country's foundations begin to decay under mismanagement, leading to a collapse like the bridge in Miami.

No Confidence
Before the rise of feminism across the world, every powerful nation thought itself superior to other nations. The Ancient Chinese thought themselves the center of the world and demanded tribute from

---

[80] Cory Booker, "The New York Fed Needs a New Perspective," *Bloomberg* (March 26, 2018).

neighboring nations. The Romans considered the Europeans to be barbarians who put butter in their hair and ran around half-naked. After subjugating the Europeans, the Romans felt they were bringing civilization to Europe. In the Colonial era, the Europeans set sail across the world and were aghast at the savages who inhabited the New World. In his famous poem "The White Man's Burden," British poet Rudyard Kipling wrote that it was the responsibility of the Europeans to civilize the "half-devil and half-child" non-Europeans.

The United States was also once confident in its values and way of life. From the ashes of World War II, we rose as the world's preeminent power and championed democracy against communism. We promoted our way of life by supporting democratic regimes throughout the world, even to the point of sending in our military in the cases of Korea and Vietnam. Through international institutions like the IMF and World Bank, we taught developing nations how to manage and grow their economies in American-style capitalism. But that has all changed in recent decades.

A growing segment of our public sees our nation and Western Civilization in general as evil. These people, who tend to be feminists, read history as a story where Europeans went across the world and subjugated colored people. They see our traditional family values, a pillar of our society, as relegating women to the degrading role of homemaker. They see our capitalistic system, which is the source of our great wealth, as a system of exploitation. These people understand the world through the feminine model of empathy.

In that model, anyone who's seen as hurting another person is wrong, regardless of the reason. They're unable to see that each person plays a different role in a greater system, where each role is meaningful but unequal in importance. An army needs generals to command and foot soldiers to fight. A general doesn't exploit foot soldiers, but they work together as a team to accomplish a goal. A foot soldier wouldn't make a good general until he gains years of experience and works his way up. A general has extensive experience and knowledge that would be wasted in a foot soldier role. The two have different roles, where one has higher status than the other has, but this status differential doesn't mean the general is bad and the foot soldier is in need of protection. It means the foot soldier is able to benefit from more experienced leadership.

But feminine empathy sees inequality as a source of exploitation rather than order. These feminists insist on demolishing our culture and replacing it with radical equality by pushing nondiscrimination, inclusivity, and the redistribution of wealth. All countries who have pursued these supposedly egalitarian principles have collapsed. In Communist China and Soviet Russia, tens of millions of people died of starvation. Only when the countries gave up on their radical egalitarian principles did the living standards of their citizens improve.

Feminists are ashamed of our culture and heritage. They stage women's events, Black history events, and Hispanic events, but they will never stage European heritage events. Instead of promoting our traditional values, we promote foreign values through diversity and inclusion efforts. Instead of spreading our way of life abroad, we dignify the barbaric customs of foreign nations as equal to our own. Yet, European culture and tradition have built the modern world. A civilization run by men would always be proud of itself, but one heavily influenced by women seems to doubt itself and apologize.

Part of the reason for this may be the tendency for women to have lower self-confidence and higher anxiety than men. The greater role feminists play in shaping our politics and culture means that their insecure nature seeps into our national dialogue. Instead of men beating foreigners to prove their superiority, we now have women apologizing to foreigners for our power, lest foreign nations feel bad about themselves.

Joseph King

No Truth
Something strange is going on across university campuses. At the University of Ottawa, yoga classes were canceled because some students were offended that white people were taking practices from an oppressed culture for their own benefit.[81] At the University of California-Berkeley, violent protests erupted to prevent right-wing pundit Milo Yiannopoulos from even speaking on campus.[82] At Northwestern University, University President Morton Shapiro openly defended racially segregated "safe spaces" because students may not be comfortable associating with people different from themselves.[83] Around half of professors in American universities provide "trigger warnings" to students of potentially disturbing material such as violence or racism.[84]

Political correctness has taken over our universities and from there moved into all aspects of our life. It

[81] Rachel Pells, "University Yoga Class Suspended Due to 'Cultural Appropriation' Dispute," *Independent* (November 22, 2015).
[82] Susan Svrluga, "UC-Berkeley Says 'Free Speech Week' Is Canceled. Milo Yiannopoulos Says He's Coming Anyway, *Washington Post* (September 23, 2017).
[83] Morton Shapiro, "I'm Northwestern's President. Here's Why Safe Spaces for Students Are Important," *The Washington Post* (January 15, 2016).
[84] Anya Kamenetz, "Half of Professors in NPR Ed Survey Have Used 'Trigger Warnings,'" *National Public Radio* (September 7, 2016).

seems there are grievance groups everywhere forcing us to apologize. This obsession with political correctness seems to stem from two sources: empathy for groups perceived as weak and a desire to be perceived as good.

The fear of offending someone has become comically large and is seen across the Western world, with ever arcane politically correct terms devised to ensure no one's feelings are hurt. In Canada, the Canadian government has mandated the use of gender-neutral pronouns like "ze" to address transgender people so zey wouldn't be offended.[85] In the UK, the government has the right to imprison people for saying offensive things on social media.[86] This ridiculous importance of not hurting anyone's feelings is a recent development that has turned into an obsession.

No man in the history of the world would ever obsess about hurt feelings in this way. One generation ago, our men were fighting the communists in the jungles of Vietnam, and two generations ago, they were storming the beaches of Normandy to save the civilized world. Men have spent most of history

---

[85] Jessica Murphy, "Toronto Professor Jordan Peterson Takes on Gender-Neutral Pronouns," *BBC News* (November 4, 2016).
[86] Susanna Rustin, "Is It Right to Jail Someone for Being Offensive on Facebook or Twitter?" *The Guardian* (June 13, 2014).

fighting and killing each other in the most wretched conditions, and even among friends, they're constantly roughing each other up. A world run by men doesn't worry about feelings getting hurt.

Typically, men and women have different priorities when they talk. Women tend to value maintaining relationships rather than honesty. A woman may express support and agreement in a conversation even if they do not agree with what's being said. Given this behavior, a woman tends to interpret disagreement as a personal offense rather than an objective view of the accuracy of what is discussed, and express disagreement as a means of personal attack. As comedian Chris Rock noted, "You cannot win in a fight against women, as men have a need to make sense."

A man is less likely to behave this way since he doesn't view disagreement as damaging a relationship. Furthermore, men tend to view discussions as a means to exchange information on activities or problems. For men, disagreement plays to their competitive nature and is an important part of a process to reach the best solution by hashing the problem out from different angles. Being nice is simply not as important to men.

But protecting someone's feelings is very important to women. Women value being "nice," and have a strong sense of empathy toward those perceived as weak. Jordan Peterson, a professor of psychology and one of the few reasonable voices in academia, constructed a series of psychological tests to determine the personality type of people who support political correctness. He found people who believed political correctness to be important tended to be female or score highly in feminine personality traits such as compassion.[87,88] The growing importance of political correctness coincides with the growing influence of feminists.

Compassion and niceness alone may give birth to political correctness, but they can't explain its growing intensity. Virtue signaling, defined as the conspicuous demonstration of moral values to enhance one's standing in a group, may be the impetus behind the radicalization of political correctness. Adherents to politically correctness seem to be continually trying to "one-up" one another to garner status within their community. For example, the election of President Trump dismayed many liberals and created a culture where Trump bashing was fashionable. Comedian Kathy Griffin went so far as to create a photoshoot of herself holding a fake, de-

---

[87] Christine Andary-Brophy, "Political Correctness: Social-Fiscal Liberalism and Left-Wing Authoritarianism," University of Toronto Department of Psychology 2015.
[88] Scott Kaufman, "The Personality of Political Correctness," *Scientific American* blogpost (November 20, 2016).

capitated gory head of Donald Trump.[89] The photo was widely condemned, but shows how a race towards virtue signaling can lead to extreme outcomes.

Conventional wisdom notes that men try to stand out from a crowd, while women prefer to standout within a crowd. This is in line with how men and women have earned their statuses throughout history. Men achieve status by accomplishing difficult deeds, while women are praised for their adherence to moral codes such as modesty and piety. Historically, men controlled the church but women were the more religious sex. In elementary school, boys horse around and drive their teacher crazy, but girls tend to seek approval by pleasing their teacher. Most men would not be interested in raising their status by demonstrating fervent adherence to a moral code, but quite a few women would. Political correctness is an avenue for women and the feminine minded to compete for status.

This competition for status is leading to increasingly absurd outcomes. Inclusivity, which on its face sounds good, has been taken to its logical extreme where even bathrooms have to labeled as gender neutral lest transsexuals become offended. The Civ-

---

[89] Libby Hill, "Kathy Griffin Shocks in Gory Photo Shoot With Donald Trump's (Fake) Head," *LA Times* (May 30, 2017).

il Rights Act of 1964 was meant to bar discrimination based on race, realizing Martin Luther King's dream where a man would be judged by the content of his character rather than the color of skin. Today, affirmative action gives black college applicants a large boost simply for being black. Schools then turn around and show off the diversity of its incoming students for good publicity.

As a nation, we're even losing our cohesion because we're afraid our values will offend others. We're afraid to proclaim English our official language, Christianity our tradition, and European our heritage because it might hurt the feelings of minorities in our country. We write public pamphlets in Spanish, say "happy holidays" instead of "merry Christmas," and put on endless multicultural celebrations. Yet, our values and heritage bind us together as a people and are responsible for our great success. When we give them up in order to make an expanding list of minorities more comfortable, we're committing national suicide.

A hysterical fear of offending other people has also led to the willful ignorance of important truths. For example, there are fewer women than men in engineering because, on average, women are less interested in engineering and not as good at math as men are. However, stating these obvious facts might hurt the feelings of some women, so they cannot be stated. Adherents of political correctness instead blame the low percentage of women in engineering on structural sexism. The fact that the gender gap in engineering widens the more egalitarian a country becomes doesn't seem to faze them. In a feminized world, some truths are too mean to be true, regardless of the evidence.

Political correctness has created a dark age in certain important fields of scientific inquiry. Substantial evidence shows that, on average, there are differences in intelligence between blacks and whites.[90] This would elegantly explain the persistent poverty of sub-Saharan African countries and the relative poverty and high crime rates of people of African descent in the U.S. and Europe. But such a fact would be hurtful to many blacks, so, instead, black poverty and crime is blamed on white racism. This has led to an ever-growing list of social programs and a sprawling bureaucracy to implement them. Yet none of these efforts have had much success because they don't address the root cause.

Our nation cannot function unless it operates on facts. We can't formulate policy unless we have an accurate understanding of a problem based on reality, rather than a set of beliefs chosen to make us feel good about ourselves. "Facts" that are based on

[90] Richard Lynn. *Race Differences in Intelligence* (Arlington, VA: Washington Summit Publishers, 2015).

feelings not only lead to ineffective policy but are also easily manipulated. Images of hard working single mothers supporting their children tug at our heartstrings and move us towards greater support of the welfare state. It would be too mean to ask these mothers to bear responsibility for their personal decisions, but without doing so, we would only have increasing numbers of single mothers.

The public shift towards valuing feelings over truth can even be seen in more mundane things like weight management. Over the past decades, our nation has become fatter. The average American woman in 2015 weighed 166lbs, which was as much as the average man did just a few decades earlier in the 1960s.[91] If overweight people lost a few pounds, they would meaningfully reduce their risk of incurring a range of life-threatening diseases and increase their attractiveness. If there were ever a social standard that needed to be enforced this seems like it would be it. But enforcement of this standard has been met with widespread opposition by women, who label it as "fat shaming." These women oppose criticizing fat people because it hurts the feelings of fat people, even though pressuring them to lose weight would lead to long-term health benefits.

---

[91] Christopher Ingraham. "The average American woman now weighs as much as the average 1960s man," *Washington Post* (June 12, 2015).

Political correctness has become so influential that it is eroding one of the most fundamental rights in our nation: the freedom of speech. Recent polling suggests that around 40% of millennials believe the government should be able to prevent people from saying statements that are offensive to minority groups.[92] This is a generational shift corresponding to the feminization of our society. This frightening view has already been implemented in the UK, where a 22-year-old British man was imprisoned for 1 year for writing hateful comments about Muslims on Facebook.[93] The suppression of speech is an attempt at thought control. It is the antithesis of freedom and everything our country stands for.

While political correctness seems to be everywhere, it's actually fragile and heavily reliant upon the apathy of the majority. Almost everything that comes out of the mouth of Donald Trump isn't politically correct, to the constant dismay of the mainstream media. Yet, Donald Trump powered on to win a general election and become President of the United States. The cries of outrage against him were shrill, but seemed to represent only a vocal minori-

---

[92] Jacob Poushter, "40% of Millennials OK With Limiting Speech Offensive to Minorities," *Pew Research* (November 20, 2015).
[93] Ashitha Nageth, "Man Jailed for Posting 'Let's Kill Every Muslim We See' on Facebook," *Metro* (September 7, 2017).

ty. Political correctness seems to owe its power more to the cowardice of the majority rather than the influence of its adherents.

Should people be able to make statements that are offensive to minority groups?

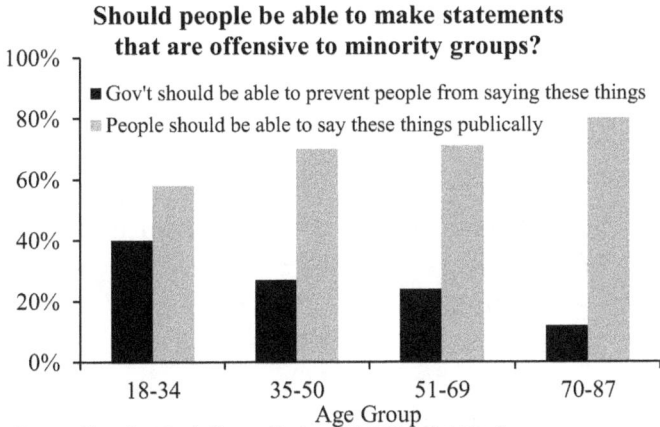

Source: Pew Research Center Spring 2015 Global Attitudes survey

Until very recently, the values of society were the values of men. Men held power and built society in their image. In a few short decades the culture of our nation, and many other countries, has shifted towards the values of women. It seems that women have become the driving force in our society. But feminine values are often at odds with masculine values. It's hard to see how a nation without a foundation in truth, without confidence in its values, that does not reward competition, and that does not respect the importance of force, can survive. The current outlook for a nation built on feminine values does not appear promising.

Joseph King

Feminist Politics

In the 20ᵗʰ century, the Western world undertook one of the most revolutionary political experiments ever – the granting of universal suffrage. For the first time in history, women were given the same political power as men. While there have always been individual female authority figures like queens, women throughout history have largely held little political power. Universal suffrage ushered in a brand new world where, for the first time, the interests and demands of women were to be accorded significant weight. These interests and demands have fundamentally altered our culture, and the course of our history.

During the first few decades following the 19ᵗʰ Amendment, women, as a whole, didn't appear to be interested in politics and had significantly lower voting turnouts than men.[94] In sharp contrast to

---

[94] Jeff Manza and Clem Brooks, "The Gender Gap in U.S. Presidential Elections: When? Why? Implications?"

today, women then leaned Republican and were actually considered more conservative than men. This pattern held until the 1980s when polling began to reveal women steadily drifting leftward towards the Democratic Party.[95] The trend of women drifting from right of center parties to left of center parties is broadly seen throughout the advanced industrialized world and continues today.

Researchers have found that those who lean left and those who lean right in their politics approach the world with a different foundational set of moral values.[96] Those who lean left tend to hold fairness and caring for the vulnerable as the two most important moral values. Those who lean right share those values, but also value in-group virtues (loyalty, patriotism etc.), hierarchal virtues (authority, obedience etc.), and sanctity virtues (respect for things that are deemed sacred). Right leaning people tend to more evenly value those five moral foundations.

American Journal of Sociology 103, no. 5 (March 1998), 1235-1266.
[95] Ronald Inglehart and Pippa Norris, "The Developmental Theory of the Gender Gap: Women's and Men's Voting Behavior in Global Perspective," *International Political Science Review* 21, no. 4 (October 2000), 441-463.
[96] Jesse Graham, Jonathan Haidt, and Brian Nosek, "Liberals and Conservatives Rely on Different Sets of Moral Foundations," *The Journal of Personality and Social Psychology* 96, no. 5 (2009), 1029-1046.

These additional moral values are essential to managing large groups, such as nation states. If we don't treat our own people better than foreigners, then a nation has no purpose. If there's no hierarchy, there's no way to organize a group of people to accomplish tasks. If we can't respect the sacred, we cannot benefit from the wisdom of our forefathers. The divide between liberal and conservative approaches to morality mirrors that of men and women, where, on average, women emphasize the personal while men emphasize the group. This is reflected in voting behavior where Democrats can be thought of as the party of the feminine minded, and Republicans the party of the masculine minded.

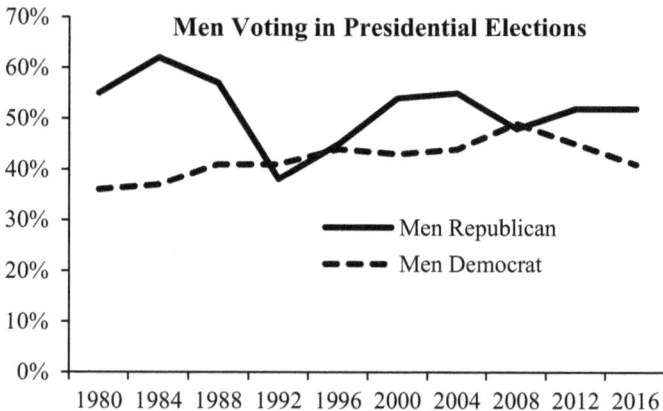

Source: Center for American Women and Politics (CAWP), Eagleton Institute of Politics, Rutgers University

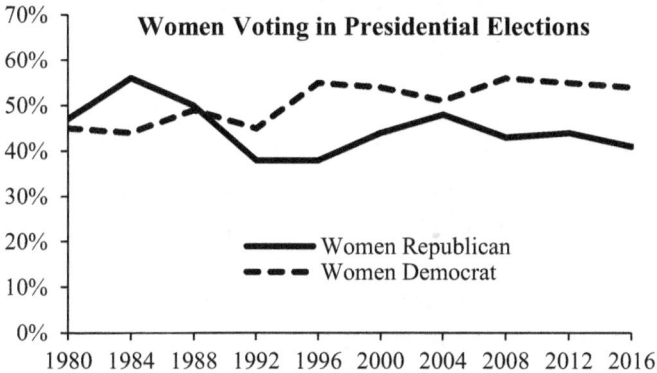

Women Voting in Presidential Elections

Source: Center for American Women and Politics (CAWP), Eagleton Institute of Politics, Rutgers University

The political gender gap that first appeared in the 1980s is today a large and important fissure in American politics. Since 1988, women have consistently expressed greater support for Democratic candidates in presidential elections. In 1985, around 43% of women thought of themselves as moderate to strong feminists, but today, that percent would no doubt be higher. The mainstream media and leading universities, both of which lean left in their politics, have been very successful in raising a generation of women in feminist beliefs. A 2015 poll suggests that 60% of women and 33% of men identify as moderate to strong feminists, though these numbers will vary depending on how the question is asked.[97]

Even before the shift in party affiliations, women had expressed policy preferences in some areas in accordance with their feminine nature. Specifically, women as a whole tended to hold policy preferences that differed from men in two key areas: force and compassion.[98] Women were significantly to the left of men on issues involving force such as gun control, capital punishment, or defense. Women were moderately to the left of men on issues involving compassion, such as public health benefits, unemployment benefits, and income redistribution.

The leftward political shift of women in the 1980s resulted in part from profound cultural shifts. More and more women began to see themselves as equal to men not just with respect to political power but in every other domain as well. The women in the early decades after universal suffrage still saw themselves as mothers and homemakers, but this new generation of women wanted to be lawyers, doctors, scientists, athletes, politician, or any other

---

[97] Weiyi Cai and Scott Clement, "What Americans Think About Feminism Today," *Washington Post* (January 27, 2016).
[98] Robert Shapiro and Harpreet Mahajan, "Gender Differences in Policy Preferences: A Summary of Trends From the 1960s to the 1980s," *The Public Opinion Quarterly* 50, no. 1 (Spring 1986), 42-61.

traditionally male-dominated job. They no longer took pride in their roles as mothers, but sought to become like men. For the first time in history, women entered the world of men and began to compete against men.

This generation of women identified themselves as feminists and boldly expressed their feminine views. The data shows that compared to men, women who identify as feminists tended to stand to the left of men on virtually all political issues. These women tended to emphasize egalitarianism, oppose racism, reject traditional moral values, and express strong sympathy to the disadvantaged. [99] In contrast, women who didn't identify as feminists held political views that are broadly similar to men. Given this dynamic it should not be surprising that our politics has become increasingly polarized as feminists have gained greater influence.

This wave of feminism was enabled by two important developments: modern contraception and the shift toward a cognitive economy. These two developments significantly equalized the innate differences between the sexes and allowed women to behave like men.

---

[99] Pamela Conover, "Feminists and the Gender Gap," *Journal of Politics* 50, no. 4 (November 1988), 985-1009.

When it comes to sex, men and women face very different costs. Sex for a man is costless, but for a woman, it could lead to pregnancy. Pregnancy would be life changing, entailing 10 months of inconvenience followed by the weighty obligation of a newborn child. If pregnancy occurred outside of marriage, it could lead to serious social stigma. Regardless, the economic and emotional costs of raising a child would be significant and difficult for a single mother to bear. These asymmetric costs meant that it was in a woman's best interest to be selective with whom she slept with. This conundrum is what underlies the concept of traditional courtship, where a man tries to win over a woman by having a good job and being a caring man.

This paradigm has been fundamentally altered by the invention of modern contraception. For the first time, sex for a woman could also be costless. In the wake of these inventions came an era of free love, which persists to this day on popular dating apps such as Tinder. Now that sex is costless, women don't have to evaluate their mates the same way they once did. This is especially true since women are now free to hold the same jobs as men and support themselves and their children. Men now also have less incentive to act in ways that demonstrate they would be good husbands.

Our movement from a labor-based economy to one based on information has nullified one of the most significant advantages men hold over women: strength. Men have significantly more upper body strength than women. Throughout history, physical strength was vitally important, whether in warfare, farming, hunting, or even working in a factory. But now, most jobs are office jobs where physical strength isn't an advantage. Many of these jobs can be performed just as well by women.

In short, advances in technology now allow women to act as if they were men. Women are represented at all levels of government, private enterprise, and even the military. They're able to engage in promiscuous sex with limited consequences. Many well-intentioned people laude these changes as progress, but social changes don't alter the fundamental psychological differences between men and women, which are grounded in biology. Women who act like men are still not men. Throughout history, men have always been the builders of nations, and women the builders of families. Managing a nation requires skills and personal qualities that are very different from managing families.

The core principal behind the political demands of feminist today seems to be this – protect the weak. In America, those perceived as weak are the illegal immigrants, homosexuals, minorities, and women.

From this springs movements towards open borders and sanctuary cities to help illegal immigrants,
civil rights to protect minorities, and political correctness to protect the feelings of the weak. These
initiatives are promulgated without any thought to
the broader impact on the nation (e.g., the significant social costs of boundless low-skilled labor).
They seem to stem out of an emotional response to
protect and nurture a perceived victim. This isn't
how a man would react, but how a mother would.

Women have built many successful families, but
never a successful nation. The growing influence of
feminists in shaping our country has eroded some
of the most basic social and political pillars upon
which our nation was built. A nation where compassion overrules reason will fall apart. This can be
seen in the relentless rise of the welfare state, and
erosion of the rule of law.

Government: A Woman's Backup Husband

America is unique in that it was founded on the
principle of limited government. Naturally, Americans were known for their strong sense of self-
reliance. When visiting the United States in the 19th
century, French political scientist Alexis de Tocqueville noted, "The citizen of the United States is
taught from his earliest infancy to rely upon his
own exertions in order to resist the evils and the
difficulties of life; he looks upon social authority

with an eye of mistrust and anxiety, and he only claims its assistance when he is quite unable to shift without it."[100]

Self-reliance is a decidedly masculine value, reflecting the rugged pioneering roots of our nation. A man is expected to support himself and his family, but a woman is expected to be supported by a man. Self-reliance also implies personal responsibility, which leads to better decision making because bad decisions have personal costs. Without this feedback mechanism, there would be no reason to learn from our mistakes and improve ourselves. Failure, though painful, is a great teacher.

The entry of women into the political realm coincides with a shift towards greater reliance on government. It may be difficult to imagine today, but a hundred years ago, the Supreme Court wouldn't even approve Federal minimum wage laws or Federal child labor laws.[101,102] This sounds cruel, but it reflects the prevailing belief of limited government at the time. Men were to take care of themselves and their families and not rely on the government. This belief in self-reliance was severely challenged by the human suffering seen during the Great Depression.

---

[100] Alexis de Tocqueville. *Democracy in America* (1835).
[101] *Adkins v. Children's Hospital*, 261 U.S. 525 (1923).
[102] *Hammer v. Dagenhart*, 247 U.S. 251 (1918).

The desperate times and changing voting demographics in the 1930s led to a rethink of the role of government. Women, though not as politically active as they are now, had become a meaningful voice in politics. President Roosevelt appointed an unprecedented number of women to high posts, including Frances Perkins as Secretary of Labor. She was the first women to ever hold a cabinet position, and an early feminist who even fought in court to keep her maiden name. By nature, women are more empathetic to the suffering of others, and are comfortable relying on others for support. True to her feminine nature, Perkins led an extensive list of New Deal programs that included vast public works projects, minimum wage laws, and social security. The Federal government, which a decade earlier couldn't mandate basic safety regulations, now shouldered the retirement obligations of the entire nation.

The effect of women's suffrage on government size can also be seen outside the Federal government. Economists John Lott and Lawrence Kenny have carefully studied the effects of women's suffrage on state government growth and found that granting women the right to vote immediately and significantly increased the size of state governments.[103]

---

[103] John Lott and Lawrence Kenny, "Did Women's Suffrage Change the Size and Scope of Government?" *Journal of Political Economy* 107, no. 6 (1999), 1163-1198.

While the 19th Amendment wasn't adopted until 1920, a number of states had been granting women the right to vote as early as the 19th century. The two economists studied how state government expenditures changed once that state granted women the right to vote. In each state, woman's suffrage led to higher government spending and a legislative body that was more in favor of government programs and regulation. The results were the same for states that had voluntarily granted women's suffrage and those who had it forced on them through the 19th Amendment, so it appears women's suffrage caused the increase in government growth.

The same phenomenon was observed across Western Europe upon the granting of universal suffrage. One study estimated that Western European countries' long run social spending increased by several percentage points of GDP due to universal suffrage.[104] Giving women the right to vote fundamentally changed the priorities and roles of government throughout the world. It seems the more political power women have, the more social services a government provides, and the more regulations there are. Women want to take care of the weak, and they're using government to do it.

---

[104] Toke Aidt and Bianca Dallal, "Female Voting Power: The Contribution of Women's Suffrage to the Growth of Social Spending in Western Europe (1869–1960)," *Public Choice* 134, nos. 3-4 (February 2008), 391-417.

Joseph King

The political gender gap in the U.S. that began in the 1980s has slowly widened over the decades. In the 2016 Presidential race, 52% of men supported Republican nominee Trump vs. 41% of women. In contrast, 54% of women supported Democratic nominee Clinton vs. 41% of men. Much of this gap has to do with alignment of feminine viewpoints with left leaning policies aimed at protecting the vulnerable, but there's also a self-interest component as well. Research shows that the risk of divorce is strongly correlated with the political gender gap.[105] As men broadly have higher incomes than women, marriage generally results in a transfer of wealth from men to women. When the risk of divorce rises, women seem to vote for higher social benefits so they would have extra income in the event of a divorce. In a sense, women vote for big government as a back-up husband.

The rise of the welfare state has made life easier for women, but it has also fundamentally undermined the traditional family. While a woman historically had to be careful in her reproductive choices, a woman today can have a child and then depend on public support. Feminist activists over the years have put in place a wide range of programs that

---

[105] Lena Edlund and Rohini Pande, "Why Have Women Become Left-Wing? The Political Gender Gap and The Decline in Marriage," *The Quarterly Journal of Economics*, 117, no. 3 (August 2002), 917-961.

help single mothers, who are often viewed as vulnerable members of society. Single mothers can qualify for food stamps, government housing, and Medicaid, among other programs. Their children can also attend public schools for free and receive subsidized meals.

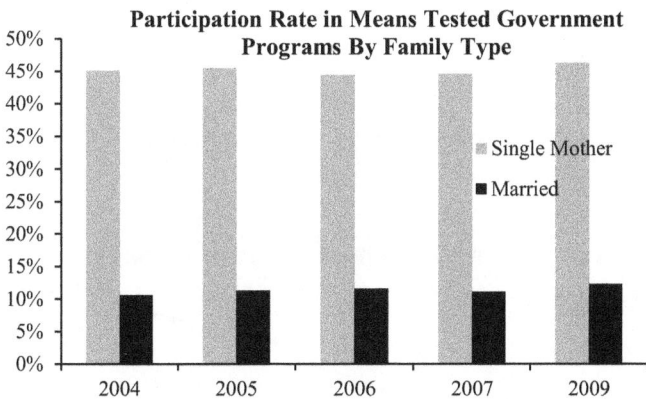

Participation Rate in Means Tested Government Programs By Family Type

Source: Kim et al. Dynamics of Economic Well-Being: Participation in Government Programs, 2004 to 2007 and 2009 Who Gets Assistance? U.S. Census Current Population Reports, July 2012.

These compassionate efforts have made life easier for single mothers, but also greatly increased their numbers. The rise of the welfare state means women don't need to be selective and date only responsible men because the Federal government will take care of them and their children. A few decades ago, single motherhood was a rare and intensely shameful status, but today, around 40% of children are born to single mothers.

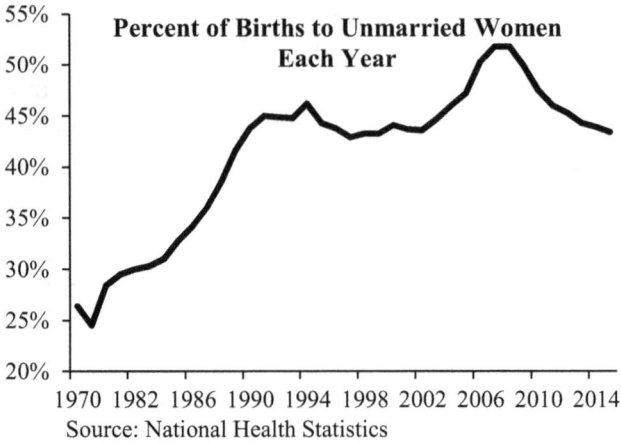

Percent of Births to Unmarried Women Each Year

Source: National Health Statistics

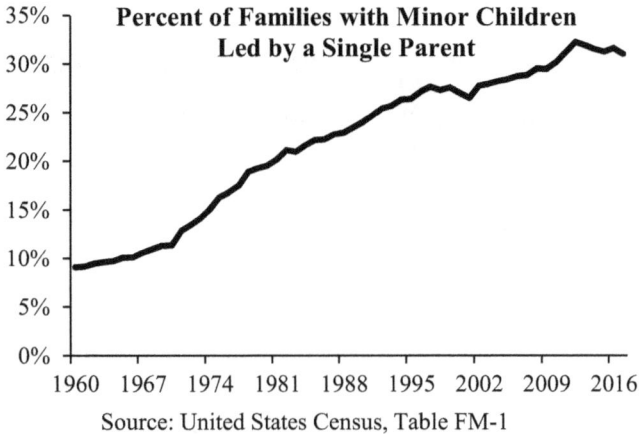

Percent of Families with Minor Children Led by a Single Parent

Source: United States Census, Table FM-1

Overall, the percent of single-parent families is steadily increasing and may one day account for the majority of family types. The vast majority of these families are led by single mothers. Many of the mothers are not divorced women, but women who were never married and sometimes even as young as teenagers. This phenomena was even glamorized in the 2007 film *Juno,* a comedy about a high school girl with an unplanned pregnancy. Single motherhood has lost it stigma and become a normal family type.

The problem with this arrangement is that children raised in single-parent households are much worse off than two-parent households. Children raised in single-parent homes have significantly higher delinquency rates, poorer grades, and higher poverty rates than children raised in two-parent households.[106] Daughters raised in single-mother households are also much more likely to become single mothers themselves, perpetuating a cycle of poverty. Raising child is a two-parent job that the government cannot replace.

---

[106] Stephen Demuth and Susan L. Brown. "Family Structure, Family Processes, and Adolescent Delinquency: The Significance of Parental Absence Versus Parental Gender," *Journal of Research in Crime and Delinquency* 41, no. 1 (February 2004), 58-81.

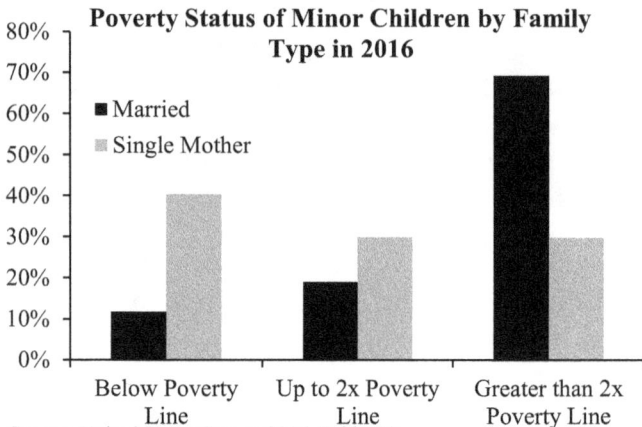

Poverty Status of Minor Children by Family Type in 2016

- Married
- Single Mother

(Categories: Below Poverty Line, Up to 2x Poverty Line, Greater than 2x Poverty Line)

Source: United States Census 2016, Table C8.

In the 2008 and 2012 election, around 75% of single moms voted for Democratic nominee Obama.[107] They are a growing voting bloc whose survival literally depends on the generosity of the public. Current trends suggest that in the near future most children will be raised by single mothers, inheriting all the disadvantages that come with such a family situation. Families are the most fundamental building block of any society, and our families are disintegrating.

Government welfare has disturbed the natural order of society by taking the pain away from poor decisions. When the costs of single motherhood

---

[107] Chris Cillizza, "Single Mothers Give Presidential Politics a New Perspective," *Washington Post* (June 2, 2013).

were starvation or social ostracization, there were very few single mothers. Feminists were empathetic to the plight of single mothers, and tried to make their lives better by offering them more government support. Their efforts helped individual single mothers, but were hurtful to our nation as a whole because it increased the number of single mothers.

The only way to end this cycle is to cut off benefits to single mothers and force them to be personally accountable for their own decisions, but that is politically impossible. Feminist voters are unable to look past the immediate pain it causes individuals to see the larger benefits to our nation. Their decision making is emotional and personal, rather than forward looking and group oriented.

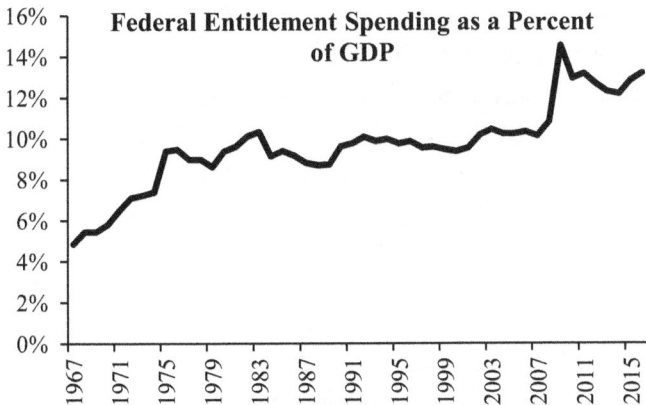

Source: Congressional Budget Office, An Update to the Budget and Economic Outlook: 2017 to 2027, June 2017

Joseph King

On a broader perspective, the national debt has exploded over the past few decades in large part because of the ever-generous benefits that have been promised to a wide range of interest groups. Inflation adjusted Federal debt per capita has gone from around $10,000 in the 1960s to over $60,000 in 2017. Today free college is a popular campaign promise, and there are even whispers of basic universal income, which is basically an allowance for everyone. The demands of those perceived as disadvantaged are ever growing, but our national income isn't unlimited.

There will eventually come a time when our welfare state becomes unsustainable and services will have to be cut. This is already happening in Europe, most notably in Greece where the elderly have had to accept deep cuts to their pensions. The Greek government broke its promise and there was nothing the elderly could do to stop them. In the U.S., the states of Illinois and California are already teetering on the brink of financial ruin largely due to the unaffordable social benefits politicians promised to buy votes. When the debt collapse eventually happens, many people who chose to rely on government rather than themselves and their own families will be devastated. This may lead to a level of social unrest on a revolutionary scale.

Inflation Adjusted Federal Debt Per Person

Source: Federal Reserve, author's calculations, 2017 dollars

With the best intentions, feminists pushed for the expansion of government to take care of everyone. But their actions had many unintended consequences. In the case of single mothers, these expanded services saved them from the consequences of their poor decisions by taking on the role of every woman's back-up husband. This led to a surge in children born to single parents, eroding our families. We are becoming a country of broken families, impoverished children, and unsustainable national debt.

Erosion of the Rule of Law
Men have a fondness for rules and laws. This can be seen even in young boys, who tend to play games that have many more rules than the games girls play. While girls are sharing their hopes and vul-

nerabilities with each other, boys are playing dungeons and dragons, soccer, softball, or some other activity governed by a set of rules. If there is conflict in a game, boys argue with each other on the basis of the rules, while girls would just abandon the game. Traditionally male dominated institutions such as the military and church have strict and elaborate codes of conduct. The court system was invented by men, and science can be thought of as an attempt by men to find laws that govern the natural world.

Laws that govern us have two components: the act of creating the law and the administration of the law. Ideally, the intent of the law created is to benefit the broader public and it's impartially administrated. Corruption arises when either the law is intended to benefit a privileged minority, or it is administrated in a way that is biased against one segment of the population. Our constitution was intended to benefit the broader public by securing for each citizen protection against tyranny through the Bill of Rights, and the establishment of a judiciary system to impartially rule on disputes. But that has gradually changed over the last century.

The rule of law is one the greatest inventions of the Western world. It means that all men would be judged by the same set of rules, rather than the whims of a king or mob. Even the king must obey the law. This implies equality before the law regardless of social standing, which provides a greater degree of legal protection to the politically unpopular. The rule of law is the absolute foundation for any personal freedom. Imagine how different life would be if you could end up in jail for being on the unpopular side of a political issue or if the politically connected could murder with impunity.

The rising power of the feminists corresponds with two developments: the creation of laws to benefit groups perceived as vulnerable, and the biased administration of neutral laws to help those same groups. As noted in earlier sections, a growing Federal government has meant more programs specifically to help select interest groups. But even facially impartial laws are also now administrated in a biased fashion to help members of groups perceived as vulnerable. In the feminine mind, justice appears to mean helping those perceived as weak regardless of their legal rights. It is a vision of justice with an intense focus on vulnerability, without any view towards the broader wellbeing of the public. The feminists intend to help the vulnerable, even at the expense of the rule of law.

The sections below highlight three recent developments where feminine empathy has led to obvious misapplications of the law: campus sexual violence, illegal immigration, and affirmative action.

Campus Sexual Assault

In November of 2016, John and Jane Doe, two students at Miami University in Ohio, went out to a bar with friends and then later engaged in sexual activity with each other.[108] The next day, Jane, who was already involved with a mutual friend, sent John text messages expressing disgust at what happened. Five months later, Jane complained to the university that she had been sexually assaulted by John, who claimed that the encounter was consensual. At the university's disciplinary panel hearing, John wasn't permitted to cross-examine any of Jane's witnesses. In fact, the panel noted that there was no need for cross-examination, since the panel already accepted her witnesses' statements as true. One panelist even suggested that the mere fact that Jane had consumed any amount of alcohol implied that she couldn't consent to sexual activity and made her a victim of sexual assault. The panel quickly determined John to be at fault and suspended him for two years.

In today's universities, a male student's life can be ruined by a baseless accusation. Indeed, many universities appear glad to demonstrate their toughness on sexual assault by harshly punishing anyone even slightly suspected of the crime. This trend be-

---

[108] Nokes v. Miami University et al., 1:17-cv-00482, Ohio Southern District Court.

gan on April 4, 2011 when the Obama's Administration's Department of Education sent a letter to all universities that detailed a new sexual assault standard. The letter mandated universities to investigate allegations of sexual assault, but also set forth procedures that significantly favored the accusers. While criminal cases require a defendant to be proved guilty "beyond a reasonable doubt," these university panels were ordered to find an accused guilty under a "preponderance of evidence" standard. That means if a panel thinks there is a 51% chance that the accused is guilty, then the panel should consider him guilty. A defendant wouldn't even have the right of cross-examining his accuser or their witnesses for fear of traumatizing the accuser by asking her to recall the details of the event.

Obama announced his bid for re-election on April 4, 2011, the same day the new sexual assault standards were announced. The Obama Administration realized toughness on sexual assault energized the feminists and was playing to win their support. Vice President Joe Biden further fanned the fantasy of a campus rape epidemic by claiming that 20% of women experienced sexual assault in college. [109] This was, of course, complete nonsense based on shoddy statistics and an extremely broad definition

[109] Glenn Kessler, "One in Five Women in College Sexually Assaulted: The Source of This Statistic," *Washington Post* (May 1, 2014).

of "sexual assault" that would include a drunken kiss at a party. But it was good politics because it fed the emotional needs of Obama's feminist base.

The Obama Administration dialed up the rhetoric where they first described the parties involved as alleged victims and alleged perpetrators, but later on simply referred to them as victims and perpetrators.[110] Along with this shift in tone came a gradual broadening of the definition of sexual violence and a movement towards a model where a single administrator would be judge, jury, and executioner in every complaint. The Obama Administration threatened to withdraw public funding from any university that did not comply with their new regulations. Universities responded by hiring increasing numbers of administrators whose job seemed to be ruling against young men. Some young men were investigated and determined to be guilty of sexual assault without even receiving written notices of the allegations filed against them.

Fortunately, Federal courts across the nation stepped in and stopped many instances of abuse by affirming each citizen's constitutional right to the due process of law. The Constitution guarantees citizens a certain set of rights when dealing with the government that include an impartial hearing, no-

---

[110] Emily Yoffe, "The Uncomfortable Truth About Campus Rape Policy" *The Atlantic* (September 6, 2017).

tice of allegations, and non-arbitrary procedures. Public universities, which are government institutions, must abide by these laws. The young men before these sex crime tribunals were not afforded these basic constitutional rights. Universities lost lawsuit after lawsuit filed by the unfortunate male students. Betsy DeVos, Secretary of Education in the Trump Administration, has also rolled back many of the sexual assault guidelines put forth by the infamous Obama Administration memo.

The sex tribunals that sprang up on campuses across the nation were kangaroo courts devoid of any sense of fairness or justice. Young women with a case of regret sex were able to destroy the lives of many young men by simply alleging sexual assault. The Obama Administration's strong desire to protect sexual assault victims led them to create rules that overwhelmingly favored accusers and undermined the fundamental rights of the accused. They were then further administrated by university panels that seemed to feel it was their duty to protect young women at all costs. Young men weren't perceived as vulnerable, so their well-being was ignored.

The high profiles of the alleged sexual assaults and relentless sexual harassment training seminars on campuses seem to have created an atmosphere of fear and paranoia among younger generations when it comes to romantic relationships. A recent poll shows that around 30% of American men and women aged 18-30 think that complimenting the appearance of someone constituted sexual harassment.[111] The same poll showed that 25% of American men aged 18-30 thought asking someone on a date was sexual harassment.

This entire panic on sexual assault was done for and with the support of Obama's feminist base. The heightened sexual assault standards were built on their belief of female victimhood and their desire to protect young women. This snowballed into mob rule under which young men where lynched at the very suggestion of sexual assault. The rule of law went out the window in a rush to protect perceived victims.

Open Borders
Deyanira's parents arrived into the U.S. illegally in search of a better life.[112] They worked hard and sent their money back to Mexico to support Deyanira and her sister. When Deyanira was 5 years old, she and her sister made the challenging trek across the border and were finally reunited with their parents.

---

[111] The Data Team, "Over-Friendly, or Sexual Harassment? It Depends Partly on Whom You Ask," *The Economist* (November 17, 2017).
[112] American Dreamers, A *New York Times* Interactive Project, accessed April 26, 2018, https://www.nytimes.com/interactive/projects/storywall/american-dreamers

Deyanira is currently a high school student with hopes of attending college, getting a good job, and realizing the American dream.

There are millions of illegal immigrants in the U.S. just like Deyanira. They're forced to live in the shadows because of their immigration status. They cannot work legally or even obtain a driver's license. President Barack Obama took these concerns to heart and in 2012 put forth the Deferred Action for Childhood Arrivals policy ("DACA"), which allowed illegal immigrants like Deyanira who came to the U.S. as minors to remain and work legally. This compassionate act gave millions of illegal immigrants, many who spent most of their life in the U.S., a real future in the U.S. But it also imposed a number of hidden costs on the American public.

The immigration debate in the U.S. has undergone a significant shift since the early 2000s. This can best seen in the evolution of Paul Krugman, a Nobel laurate in economics and left-wing pundit. He wrote in 2006 that our country needed better control of illegal immigration because illegal immigrants took more out of the social safety net than they paid in and because they depressed the wages of low skilled Americans.[113] In 2017, Paul Krugman wrote another column on illegal immigration, this

---

[113] Paul Krugman, "North of the Border," *New York Times* (March 27, 2006).

time, refuting his earlier statements and suggesting that anyone who opposed illegal immigration was racist.[114] The Democratic Party now goes so far as to even reject the idea of illegal immigration by simply referring to illegal immigrants as "immigrants."[115]

This embrace of boundless illegal immigration is a clear disregard for the rule of law. Some progressive run cities like San Francisco have even declared themselves "sanctuary cities" where they outright refuse to enforce federal immigration law.[116] In New York City, many of the menial jobs such as delivery guys or kitchen assistants are held by illegal immigrants, yet there are virtually no deportations. The number of illegal immigrants in the city was estimated to be an eye popping 500,000 in 2007.[117] The city government appears to openly support illegal immigration, where city agencies even state that they will offer services regardless of immigration status.

---

[114] Paul Krugman, "Dreamers, Liars and Bad Economics," *New York Times* (September 8, 2017).
[115] Peter Beineart, "How the Democrats Lost Their Way on Immigration," *The Atlantic* (July/August 2017).
[116] Christina Littlefield, "Sanctuary Cities: How Kathryn Steinle's Death Intensified the Immigration Debate," *LA Times* (July 24, 2015).
[117] Fiscal Policy Institute, *Working for a Better Life: A Profile of Immigrants in the New York State Economy* (2007).

This defiance of the rule of law isn't just due to strong feelings of empathy, but also seems to stem from a wholesale rejection of the idea of nationhood. This can be seen in the views of the supporters of illegal immigration. Many of them protest the construction of a border wall along Mexico as racist, and strongly support granting the beneficiaries of DACA not just the right to work but a path towards citizenship. Illegal immigrants themselves even show up at protests openly demanding a right to stay in our country.[118] One popular protest sign reads, "No human is illegal," suggesting that being human gives people the right to live anywhere they want.

The overarching idea seems to be an attempt to replace nationhood in favor of a unity bound by common humanity. This is unprecedented and alien to male nature. Men instinctively see themselves as part of a tribe and seek to advance the interests of their own tribes, even if it's at the expense of foreigners. The long the brutal history of warfare is the best proof for this behavior. Throughout history, men have stood in battlefields risking life and limb for the survival and glory of their tribe. The Israelites fought the Canaanites, the Romans fought the Carthaginians, the Americans fought the Ger-

---

[118] Justin Moyer and Maria Sacchetti, "Disappointed Advocates Rally, Vent While 'Dreamers' Hang in the Balance," *Washington Post* (January 23, 2018).

mans and Japanese, and so forth. Embedded in every struggle is a respect for a man's tribe that's greater than a man's own life. After all, if his tribe is defeated, then he'll lose everything. Nationhood is a masculine idea.

While men died for their tribe, women stayed at home in safety. If their men were victorious, all would be well; if not, then the enemy would take them and their children captive. Women survived in either case, though their lives would likely be worse as captives. A woman's focus has never been the protection of her tribe, but the survival of her family.

The growing cultural movement towards unity based on common humanity and its corresponding political shift towards open border policies is exactly what would be expected in a feminized society. Compared to men, women have a weaker sense of in-group loyalty and a stronger sense of empathy. Women instinctively react strongly to the human suffering they see in illegal immigrants. They perceive the illegal immigrant to be more vulnerable than their own fellow citizens, and, accordingly, decide in favor of them regardless of the law or costs illegal immigration has on the American public.

The costs of illegal immigration are clear and straightforward: lower wages, higher social expenditures, and weaker communities. From a basic supply and demand viewpoint, an increase in cheap labor drives down the level of wages. The entrance of tens of millions of illegal immigrants into the labor force means that unskilled Americans face tougher competition, and lower wages. Furthermore, these illegal immigrants use far more public services than they pay in taxes. Illegal immigrants tend to work off the books and have low income, so they likely pay very little in taxes. Yet they send their children to schools, get free healthcare, benefit from police and firefighter protection, and use public infrastructure like roads. Research suggests that the average IQ of the illegal immigrants is meaningfully lower than the average white American, and this IQ gap will persist for generations, as IQ is in part hereditary.[119] It seems that, on average, illegal immigrants and their children will continue to take more out of public services than they pay in taxes. This means that Americans will have to pay more taxes to support them and their children for generations to come.

Research and commonsense suggest that cultural diversity undermines social cohesion. [120] People

---

[119] Jason Richwine, "IQ and Immigration Policy. Harvard University" (PhD diss., Harvard Kennedy School of Government, 2009).
[120] Robert Putnam, "E Pluribus Unum: Diversity and Community in the Twenty-First Century – The 2006

Joseph King

trust other people who hold the same beliefs as they do. A multicultural society is one where Arabic-speaking Muslims, Spanish-speaking Mexicans, and English-speaking Americans all live in the same neighborhood; it's a society where no one has anything in common with one another. It should be obvious that without mutual trust and understanding, the level of social interaction between people becomes strained. In this kind of low-trust society, people feel isolated, crime rises, and the quality of life declines.

American immigration laws were made to benefit Americans. They help protect the jobs of our poorest and most vulnerable citizens, and maintain our cultural cohesion. An open disregard for our immigration laws in favor of open borders helps poor foreigners at the expense of poor Americans. Feminists seem to feel more sorry for the third world poor than the American poor, so they happily disregard immigration laws to help those they perceive to be the weakest. To them, it makes little difference whether someone is American or foreign. Men help those who are part of their tribe, but women help whomever is most vulnerable.

Johan Skytte Prize Lecture," *Scandinavian Political Studies* (June 2007).

Affirmative Action

Affirmative action is the policy of giving members of certain demographic groups an advantage when it comes to school admissions or job applications. Giving preferences to a person based solely on race or sex is obviously not only racist and sexist but also in violation of the plain text of the law. Under Title VI of the Civil Rights Act of 1964, employers are prohibited from discriminating based on race or sex. Under the Equal Protection Clause of the 14th Amendment, Federal and state governments are not allowed to discriminate based on race or sex. Notwithstanding these facts, affirmative action has, over the decades, become an accepted facet of our society.

The rise of affirmative action corresponds with the rise of feminism. Feminists have long viewed minorities as victims in need of extra help. When their empathy-driven sense of fairness ran afoul of the law, they pushed for the law to be bent. President Obama even proclaimed empathy to be an important quality in a judge on the Supreme Court.[121] He subsequently appointed two women, Justices Kagan and Sotomayer, to the Court. Both women have consistently supported affirmative action policies, as has Justice Ruth Ginsberg.

---

[121] Peter Slevin, "In Filling Supreme Court Vacancy, Obama Looks for a Jurist With Empathy," *The Washington Post* (May 13, 2009).

While the courts have stood up against the Obama Administration's kangaroo campus sex tribunals, they affirmed the legality of affirmative action, beginning with the *Bakke* case in 1978. Allan Bakke, a former U.S. Marine Corp Officer, applied for and was rejected by the University of California at Davis's Medical School. Bakke discovered that he was more qualified than every minority admitted under Davis' quota-based affirmative action program that year, and asserted that he was denied admission solely because he was white in violation of the Equal Protection clause of the 14th Amendment. The Supreme Court sided with Bakke and ruled that racial quotas were unconstitutional, but also held that a university could take race into account when judging an applicant. Racial diversity was a considered a valid goal in an educational setting.

Bakke signaled that affirmative action could be legal if applied in a less cumbersome way. This may have been an understandable ruling at the time, when the nation was adjusting to a post-segregation world. Justice Blackmun even suggested in his concurring *Bakke* opinion that the policy would be temporary. But the Court continued to support the policy a generation later in a pair of decisions involving the University of Michigan. In *Gratz vs. Bollinger* (2003), the Court found Michigan's point-based system for undergraduate admissions to be unconstitutional. Under the system, an applicant who achieved an admissions score of 100 would be automatically admitted, but racial minorities were automatically awarded 20 points. In contrast, a perfect SAT score was only worth 12 points.[122] This blunt treatment of race was regarded as unconstitutional, in line with *Bakke*.

In the same year, the Court upheld the University of Michigan Law School's affirmative action program in *Grutter v. Bollinger*. The main difference between the two cases was how racial preferences were applied. Instead of a mechanical point system, the Law School claimed to use race in a more holistic case-by-case way. Justice O'Connor, who wrote the majority opinion for the Court, ruled that diversity in the context of education was an important enough reason to justify racial preferences. This view was re-affirmed by the Court as recently as 2016 in *Fisher v. University of Texas*.

Affirmative action programs by private companies have also been upheld by the Court despite their obvious violation of Title VI of the Civil Rights Act.[123] The rationale the Court gave centered not on the educational benefits of diversity, but the im-

---

[122] Carolyn Gearig, "Gratz Speaks at North Quad, Reflects on 2003 Affirmative Action Case," *The Daily Michigan* (October 22, 2013).
[123] *United Steelworkers v. Weber* (1979); *Johnson v. Transportation Agency, Santa Clara County* (1987).

portance of remediating past discrimination. The Court noted that an affirmative action program would be compliant with Title VI if the program was aimed at remediating past discrimination, was temporary, and would not unduly burden the rights of those who did not benefit from the program. Interestingly, private sector employers defend their affirmative action programs today by claiming that diversity is good for business. The Court hasn't ruled on private sector affirmative action programs since 1987, and it has never affirmed a private sector affirmative action program whose basis for discrimination was to promote diversity and inclusion.

It's hard to say who has been helped by affirmative action. Proponents of affirmative action point to higher minority enrollment in universities as a sign of its success, but research suggests that students admitted under affirmative action struggle academically, with most ending up at the bottom 10% of their class.[124] These students are placed in an academic environment above what their credentials merit, so they have trouble keeping pace with other students. Affirmative action seems to undermine the self-esteem of its beneficiaries, reinforcing negative stereotypes, and discriminate against applicants who would have otherwise been admitted.

---

[124] Richard Sander, "A Systemic Analysis of Affirmative Action in American Law Schools," *Stanford Law Review* 57, no. 367 (November 2004), 368-478.

Affirmative action programs have also been unpopular with many voters. A Quinnipac poll found that a majority of Americans, especially men, disagreed with the policy.[125] Eight states have banned affirmative action, either through ballot initiatives or the state legislature.[126] The policy itself obviously clashes with the race blind and sex blind ideal taught in our culture. It also clashes with the masculine ideas of competition by replacing merit with demographic membership.

Affirmative action programs were initially viewed as temporary programs to facilitate minority integration. But racial achievement gaps persist despite 50 years of affirmative action, even as society as a whole has become a lot less racist. There is substantial evidence that suggests the gap isn't due to racism, but a reflection of differences in average ability between the races.[127] Affirmative action today has become another welfare program that's meant to help those perceived as disadvantaged. With feminists groups agitating for more special treatment for minorities, and three feminists sitting on

---

[125] Quinnipiac poll conducted on June 3, 2009.
[126] The states are Oklahoma, New Hampshire, Arizona, Nebraska, Michigan, Florida, Washington, and California.
[127] Joseph King. *Awake: An Introduction to New Nationalism* (New Nationalists, 2017).

the Supreme Court, it looks like these obviously illegal programs will continue.

The Rule of Law

The rule of law means each person is equal before
the law, regardless of wealth, race, sex, or any other
status. It implies an impartial administration of the
law, irrespective of how sympathetic a person or a
group of people are. Over the past decades, the rule
of law has steadily been subverted in favor of those
perceived as weak. Feminists, who are longtime
supporters of women and racial minorities, have
successfully pushed policies that violate the fundamental right of equality before the law that the
Constitution was meant to protect. In their quest to
mother the weak, they have eroded one of the
founding pillars of our nation.

In the eyes of feminists, empathy supersedes justice.
If feminists ruled the world, then our immigration
policy would be designed to help poor people from
third world countries improve their lives by immi-
grating here. This would drive down wages for our
own people, and place an unsustainable burden upon our schools and other public institutions. These
low-skilled immigrants could barely survive in their
own country, and would never pay more in taxes
than what they took out. If feminists ruled the
world, then our justice system would be a giant
scale weighing perceived victimhood. This would

trample the rights of those perceived as privileged and lead to tyranny by perceived victims. If feminists ruled the world, then admission, hiring, and promotion decisions would be based on helping those perceived as disadvantaged. This would undermine all our institutions because we would not be choosing our leaders for their talent and competence, but on identity politics. Our most talented people would not be able to exercise their talents.

There have been countless civilizations across the world and across time, but not one of them has been built by women. The feminine principle of empathy over justice would be a good fit for taking care of a group of children, but unworkable as a principle for governing a nation. Empathy invites subjectivity, which is the complete opposite of the rule of law. If feminists ruled the world, there would be no laws and, thus, no civilization.

Joseph King

Women as Warriors

The 1980s hit movie series *Star Wars* was a story about young Jedi Luke Skywalker and his band of largely male heroes fighting the Empire and saving the universe. Recent additions to the *Star Wars* franchise cast a female as the lead warrior among a largely female led rebellion army struggling to save the universe. *Ghostbusters,* another hit 1980s movie series, was a story about four men in New York City who teamed up to save the city from terrible supernatural evils. The 2016 remake of the movie cast four women as the lead protagonists. The message is clear: women can be warriors just like men.

What is being reflected in mainstream movies is the ultimate conclusion of a decades-long effort to masculinize women. This began by allowing women into the workplace, a domain previously dominated by men. Once that was achieved, feminists campaigned for entry into all fields that historically belonged to men. Competitive team sports, long a historic pastime of men, would soon see an inflow of women. Title IX, a civil rights law passed in 1972, mandated publically funded schools to create athletic programs for women. Some private sector entities even went further created professional women's sports leagues such as the WNBA and Women's United Soccer Association. In 2015, women gained entry into the last male dominated domain: military combat roles.[128]

The message is clear – woman can also be strong, independent, and courageous. Women can also be warriors. More importantly, women *should* be warriors.

Before the 1960s, most women were homemakers. Their job was to take care of the kids while their husbands worked outside the home. Surveys on the happiness of housewives conducted in those times consistently showed women to be happy with their life choices with little desire of becoming a professional woman.[129] Our culture had followed a traditional division of labor that has existed since the dawn of time: men provide while women look after the children.

---

[128] Rosenberg and Phillips, "All Combat Roles Now Open to Women, Defense Secretary Says," *New York Times* (December 3, 2015).
[129] Charles Murray. *Coming Apart, The State of White America, 1960-2010* (2012).

The masculinization of women was largely led by a vocal and determined group of feminist women. Despite being a minority among women, these feminist women have been able to influence the social norms and structure of our entire society. Their work has been a disaster for two reasons. First, women simply aren't very good at being men. The performance of women in historically male dominated domains is poor and there is little reason to expect improvement. Secondly, it has eroded our families. When women are taught to become men, then they don't become good mothers.

Fake Men

In 2013, Sheryl Sandberg wrote a best-selling career advice book for women titled *Lean in: Women, Work, and the Will to Lead*. The book essentially notes that women would be more professionally successful if they were more confident, aggressive, and ambitious. In a nutshell, women would be more professionally successful if they were more masculine. Sandberg predictably downplays the biological differences between the sexes and emphasizes the cultural conditioning each sex receives. Ironically, Sandberg's own life experiences illustrate the biology-based differences between the sexes discussed in earlier chapters. When Sandberg was in business school, she was awarded a prize, split among six students, for high academic achievement. The other five students, all men, disclosed their winnings, but Sandberg kept her award a secret. When *Forbes* ranked Sandberg as one of the world's most powerful women, she "felt embarrassed and exposed."[130] Men are programmed to seek high status and are comfortable with hierarchy, but women aren't.

Despite a strong push towards the masculinization of women, there aren't many women in top leadership roles in politics or industry. Women account for 57% of college graduates and are given affirmative action boosts in many companies, yet only 5% of Fortune 500 companies are run by women.[131,132] There are several reasons for this, but most of it stems from the fact that, on average, women aren't the same as men. One study by professors at Harvard Business School found that women are simply less interested than men in climbing the professional ladder. Compared to men, they place greater weight on other life goals such as marriage and family, and they're more concerned about the conflict that comes with promotions.[133] To rise profes-

[130] Amy Alkon, "Science Says 'Lean In' Is Filled With Flawed Advice, Likely to Hurt Women," *Observer* (May 15, 2015).

[131] National Center for Education Statistics, Table 318.30.

[132] Caroline Fairchild, "Why so Few Women Are CEOs (in 5 Charts)," *Fortune* (January 14, 2015).

[133] Francesca Gino et al., "Compared to Men, Women View Professional Advancement as Equally Attainable, But Less Desirable," *PNAS* 112, no. 40 (September 2015).

sionally increases one's status and power, but it takes a lot of sacrifice. One has to spend more time at work, take risks, and make enemies. Most women would rather have a less prestigious but stable job that gives them time to watch their children grow up.

That's not at all to say there should be no female leaders in industry, but only to note that the science suggests there would be proportionately fewer women in high level positions. There's a significant amount of variation across individuals, such that there will always be women who are very ambitious, team oriented, and talented. But statistically, the vast majority of people who have both the talent and interest in C-suite positions will be men. That is precisely what we see in real life.

But even in these conditions, something weird and unnatural is happening: men are competing with women. Before feminism, men and women inhabited different spheres and were never in direct competition with one another. Men know how to compete with each other; they talk trash, interrupt each other, and boast when they win. Men don't take any of these actions too seriously, but treating a woman competitor that way would likely lead to anger and hurt feelings. Men don't really know how to compete with women, but are now forced to. This has led to bizarre group dynamics and unnecessary conflict. Furthermore, women demand all sorts of benefits like maternity leave, flexible work arrangements, or childcare. It seems that the entire professional world was remade just so a minority of feminist women would better be able to compete with men.

The dominance of men remains particularly strong in a few important industries. Biological differences between the sexes suggests that there would be strong sex segregation across industries, where women are more strongly represented in industries dealing with people and men more strongly represented in industries dealing with things. This is exactly what we see in fields such as engineering and nursing. Even the massive pushes towards gender equality undertaken in Scandinavia couldn't change this pattern. The male dominated fields such as science and technology are the fields that have been changing the world. The difference between us and the African bushman is our science and technology, which continues to be largely a product of men. Despite all the noise made by feminists, at the end of the day, it's still men who are changing the world.

In politics, women have also not been very successful. A majority of Americans are women, but women make up only 20% of Congress.[134] The factors that lead to fewer women CEOs also lead to fewer women political leaders. Politics is a high status, hierarchal, and intensely stressful game where political opponents aren't above unearthing the most embarrassing details of someone's life. Many more men than women are interested in playing that game.

The performance of women as men isn't just about representation in male dominated industries, but also about the performance of women who hold jobs traditionally held by men. This is because representation of women in many areas is artificially boosted because of affirmative action, where a woman is hired largely because she's a woman. But there's a good chance that women who hold roles in the private sector do a reasonable job. A corporation has a clear goal: to make money. A company may hire a woman based on diversity and affirmative action, but she has to contribute to the bottom line to remain. The women who remain likely made the cut.

This would not be true in the public sector, where incompetent women can hold positions because it's good politics. Justice Sotomayer, a woman with

---

[134] Rutgers Eagleton Institute of Politics, Center for American Women and Politics, Factsheet as of March 2018.

remarkably unremarkable accomplishments, was named to the Supreme Court by President Obama, no doubt in large part, because she was a Hispanic woman. By her own admission, her academic and professional accomplishments were due to affirmative action.[135] Based on merit, the position would have likely gone to a man. But Obama was intent on maintaining the illusion that women are just like men, and chose a woman. Sotomayer's performance on the Court has largely been an embarrassment, and the public at large is suffering from a less competent Supreme Court. There are many women just like Sotomayer in the public sector where their incompetence is shielded from accountability.

The 19th Amendment granted women entry into the traditionally male dominated world of politics, but they've exercised that privilege poorly. Women have used their vote to support policies more in line with their feminine values. While feminine values are well suited to managing a family, they are dysfunctional when applied to a nation. In previous chapters, I've outlined how the rise of feminism correlates to the rise in the welfare state and erosion of the rule of law in this country. But the same phenomena can be seen worldwide.

---

[135] Bill Mears, "Sotomayor Says She Was 'Perfect Affirmative Action Baby,'" *CNN* (June 11, 2009).

At the time of this writing, Angela Merkel, Prime Minister of Germany, is the most influential female leader in the world. Her signature policy is the importation of over two million Muslim refugees, most of whom are unskilled and don't speak any German. This is an act of kindness intended to alleviate human suffering, but has had a significantly negative impact on Germany. These refugees, who are predominately young men, have led to a surge in crime throughout Germany.[136] Rates of sexual assault have skyrocketed and refugee ghettoes that are virtually under sharia law have emerged. These ghettoes are known as "no-go" zones because even the police are afraid of entering.[137] When men ruled Europe, they realized that the Muslims were a threat to their civilization and fought them for hundreds of years. Now women are welcoming these alien and likely unassimilable people into their country. Ironically, if the Muslims had their way, then German women would be required to wear veils in public and be housewives. Would Germany still be Germany if it became Muslim?

The recent trend of multiculturalism is another good example of feminine values influencing our

---

[136] *BBC* Staff, "Germany: Migrants 'May Have Fueled Violent Crime Rise,'" *BBC* (January 3, 2018).
[137] Sebastian Murphy-Bates, "Angela Merkel Admits There ARE 'No-Go' Area in Germany That 'Nobody Dares' to Enter," *Daily Mail* (February 28, 2018).

national politics. A multicultural nation is not a nation, but a group of people sharing the same piece of land. Men have always had a clear sense of group loyalty and group values, where much of history is one group of men killing or ruling over a foreign group. But women, being egalitarian and empathetic, want everyone to feel welcome. The male solution to foreigners has been to apply hierarchy and dominate the other group, but the female solution is to welcome them and treat them as equals. Men would demand immigrants to assimilate and take on the values of their new country. This is not to say that multiculturalism has no value, but taken to the levels seen today, it's simply chaos and cultural suicide.

The efforts toward the masculinization of women have failed most spectacularly when it comes to areas relating to physical differences between the sexes. Feminists set their eyes on the male-dominated area of professional sports as an area of inequality and sought to create sports leagues for women. But professional sports leagues for women have been huge failures. The WNBA has been around for over two decades and it's still struggling financially, where half of its 12 teams lost money in 2016.[138] The truth is that people don't like watching compet-

---

[138] Richard Sandomir, "After Two Decades, W.N.B.A. Still Struggling For Relevance," *New York Times* (May 28, 2016).

itive women's sports because they just aren't as good as the male professional players. For example, the U.S. women's Olympic hockey team scrimmages with high school men's varsity team for practice and regularly loses.[139] The U.S. women's national soccer team, which has won four Olympic gold medals, can also be easily beaten by a high school men's Under 15 team.[140]

The entry of women into military combat roles has forced the U.S. Army to lower physical fitness standards. In 2018, the U.S. Army announced it would give up the requirement that recruits throw a grenade 25 meters because many recruits couldn't meet the requirement.[141] Even the staunchest deniers of biological differences between men and women acknowledge that there's a very large gap between the throwing abilities of men and wom-

---

[139] Ben Rohrbach, "U.S. Women's Hockey Team Scrimmaging Against High School Boys With Mixed Results," *Yahoo Sports* (January 10, 2014).
[140] Will Griffe, "From World Champions to Humbling Defeat Against Under 15s Side... World Cup-Winning USA Women's Team Suffer 5-2 Loss Against Dallas Academy Boys," *Daily Mail* (April 7, 2017).
[141] Ariel Zilber, "US Army Drops Grenade Throwing as a Requirement to Graduate Because New Recruits Can't Throw Far Enough (But Do They Mean Women?)" *Daily Mail* (February 15, 2018).

en.[142] In fact, the "throwing gap" may be the largest physical sex difference between men and women. Men are able to throw things farther, faster, and more accurately than women. It seems the entry of women into the military can only be made possible by lowering our recruitment standards.

Men have long worked in groups to tackle life-threatening situations, such fighting off enemies or avoiding starvation. To meet these challenges, men have evolved to be physically stronger, more resilient to emotional stress, aggressive, as well as have an instinctive sense of hierarchy. In contrast, women have never had to face these challenges. Compared to the average man, the average woman is more risk averse, physically weaker, and less ambitious. The average woman, when judged by male standards, would be a loser.

The clear biological differences between men and women suggest that, on average, men will continue to hold more leadership roles and have higher representation in certain industries. To suggest otherwise would only create fake claims of discrimination that ferment social unrest. The same pattern is seen throughout history: virtually all great people have been men. From Copernicus to Martin Luther

[142] Janet Hyde, "The Gender Similarities Hypothesis," *American Psychologist* 60, no. 6 (September 2005), 581-592.

 the

to Abraham Lincoln, men have always been the ones who possess both the originality and courage to change the world. No amount of social engineering or discrimination laws can change this biological reality. Women don't make good men.

Woman of the House
The most basic building block of any nation is the family. Families support and socialize children, who are the future of any nation. A functioning family takes care of the physical needs of its children and invests in them so that they grow up to be self-supporting adults. Over the past years, our families have disintegrated to the point where now close to half of children are born to single mothers. Statistically, children who grow up in single parent homes have higher rates of poverty and delinquency. They're also much more likely to later become single parents themselves, perpetuating the cycle of crime and poverty. Public welfare hasn't been an adequate substitute for two parents. The decay of our families happened recently, rapidly, and in the same timeframe as the rise in feminism.

When feminists gained influence, they sought to make women equal not only in the professional world but also in the personal realm. The ultimate dream of the feminists seems not just to have equal legal rights as men but to become men. Feminist shows like the hit series *Sex and the City* glamorize women who pursue casual relationships, engage in promiscuous sex, and seek high-powered careers. The protagonists are basically women who act as if they were men. But feminist media doesn't portray the sacrifices and joy of motherhood. Unsurprisingly, many early feminists viewed motherhood as a form of social control by men.[143] Prominent feminists like Simone de Beauvoir and Gloria Steinem never had children. Shulamith Firestone even remarked that "pregnancy is barbaric"; childbirth is "like shitting a pumpkin"; and childhood is "a supervised nightmare."[144]

Recent feminists seem more accepting of the biological act of bearing children, but continue to regard the social role of motherhood negatively. In their eyes, being a mom is simply not as good as being a career woman. One prominent feminist has even suggested that it should be illegal to be a stay-at-home mom as a way to promote gender equality.[145] This is all understandable, since pregnancy and motherhood would completely shatter the feminists' illusion that she could be a man. Notwith-

---

[143] Gerda Neyer and Laura Bernardi, "Feminist Perspectives on Motherhood and Reproduction," *Historical Social Research* 36, no 2 (January 2011), 162-176.
[144] Susan Faludi, "Death of a Revolutionary," *New Yorker* (April 15, 2013).
[145] Sarrah Le Marquand, "It Should Be Illegal to Be a Stay-at-Home Mum," *The Daily Telegraph* (March 20, 2017).

Joseph King

standing the obvious absurdity, feminists have largely won the cultural war and succeeded in convincing our young women that they should act like men.

In the early 1960s, Gallup polled 1,813 women on whether it would be appropriate for a woman to have premarital sex with a man that she was going to marry. Eighty-six percent of these women said it wouldn't be appropriate.[146] It's likely that the same poll conducted today would return a result closer to zero percent, with a majority open to sex with someone they barely know. This shift in social norms with respect to female promiscuity is without precedent in human history. Obviously, it has been a primary reason for the increase in single mothers. But the shift in social norms has also upended historical dating conventions in ways that further damage the family unit.

Feminism has meant that women are having fewer children, and that more of those children are being born to single mothers. The impact of feminism on childbearing is a different story for smart and dumb women. These are just rough categories created to make a point. Roughly speaking, smart women are talented, responsible, and come from supportive families. Dumb women come from less fortunate backgrounds and aren't as responsible. Under fem-

---

[146] Murray, 164.

inism, smart women have been able to pursue the high-powered careers their mothers dreamed of, but at the cost of having fewer or no children. Dumb women have gained the freedom to more easily become pregnant.

For a smart woman, the world has never been better. Every professional door is open to her, and, in many cases, she receives a bump through affirmative action. Despite the strong movement towards equality of the sexes, she continues to receive the courtesies and privileges traditionally accorded to women as the weaker sex. Men open doors for her, pay for her dinners, and fight the nation's wars for her. The strongest supporters of feminism are often found among these smart women. She follows the standard path of college, graduate school, and then work, but here, biological reality reveals itself.

While feminists teach young women they can do anything men can, a woman's biological clock states otherwise. Women have a more limited window of fertility than men have. Until very recently, young women were virtually all mothers by their early 20s. Young men at the time were expected to go to college or graduate school and then establish themselves professionally. Women today, especially smart women, are expected undertake the same track as men and postpone marriage for career and graduate school. Many smart women don't have children until their 30s, sometimes only with the help of fertility clinics. They try to follow a man's life path, but at the expense of their fertility. Instead of having babies, these professional women end up raising dogs or cats.

For dumber women, feminism has not opened up more doors. They work the menial jobs they would have in days past, but have the freedom to behave as men. Many of them exercised their freedom in a way that results in pregnancy and dependency on public welfare. Our traditional cultural norms would have prevented these outcomes, but those norms have been swept away. A generation ago, our society taught women to only have sex when they're married, but today, we teach 14-year-old girls how to have "safe sex." A couple generations ago, being a single mom was a rare and shameful thing, but now, it has lost its stigma. These factors have led to a surge of single moms among dumb women.

This shift in norms is itself a reflection of the feminization of society, in which morality is based on empathy instead of adherence to rules designed to benefit the larger group. Instead of being viewed as morally reprehensible for violating social rules, single moms are now viewed as vulnerable members of society who require our protection. Single mothers today receive billions in subsidized medical care, food, and education. They seem more likely to receive words of support than condemnation. As there are far more dumb women than smart women, a growing number of children are born to single mothers.

Adherence to traditional social rules would have meant a rough life for single moms, but it would have also meant fewer single moms. When men ruled the world, they set rules with an eye towards benefiting the nation as a whole. But women set rules with a focus on the suffering of individuals rather than broader future implications. To accommodate a vulnerable minority, we have created a system that enables single motherhood and negatively affects the welfare of our nation.

The rise of nontraditional families is due to not only the choices of women but also those of men. A man can choose to stay with a woman and raise their child together. A few decades ago, a woman wouldn't have sex with a man if she didn't feel that he would be emotionally invested in her and her child. As noted earlier, the rise of the welfare state has made the commitment of men less important to a woman. Women are also more able to find jobs and support themselves. These developments have both raised and lowered the standards of men who succeed in dating.

The large-scale entrance of women into the workforce ushered in profound changes in our economy.

On the most basic level, higher participation of women in the labor force meant a significant increase in workers looking for jobs. Economists have shown that this increased supply of labor led to both lower wages for men and women.[147] Men who worked in middle-skilled office jobs were particularly affected, since women tended to work in those jobs. A few decades ago, a man could support his family with a single income, but today, many families require two incomes to stay afloat.

Traditional courtship practices are built on the principles of men as providers. On dates, men are expected to pay for women and shower them with gifts. A woman's engagement ring is expected to be months of a man's salary. A man is expected to have a stable job or, at the very least, be able to support himself. These are signals meant to show a woman that her suiter would be a good provider. A woman continues to expect a man to earn more than she does, but that's increasingly difficult for many men. An increasingly large swath of men can longer hope to attract a woman by being a provider.

The labor participation rate of women steadily rose in the first half of the 20th century as more women

---

[147] Davon Acemoglu, David H. Autor, and David Lyle, "Women, War, and Wages: The Effect of Female Labor Supply on the Wage Structure at Midcentury," *Journal of Political Economy* 112, no. 3 (2004), 497-551.

entered the labor force, but, at the same time, the labor participation rate of men steadily declined. The decline in male labor participation is due to a number of factors, including the decline of male dominated fields such as manufacturing, but is also due in part to women taking their jobs. With government stepping into the role of husband for the poorest women and many women replacing middle income men, fewer men are able to play traditional masculine roles. A growing population of single, unemployable men is a recipe for social unrest.

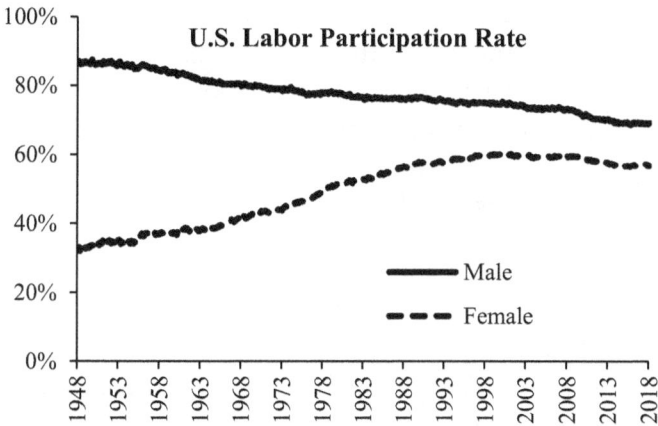

U.S. Labor Participation Rate

Source: Federal Reserve

This apparent obsolescence of men as providers has shifted the way a man is judged by a woman; a man is now more heavily judged on his physical attractiveness than he has been in earlier periods. For a man, the value in the dating market of having stable job has declined while the value of being tall, handsome, and muscular has significantly risen. He is now judged as if he were a woman. At the same time, values women traditionally looked for such as commitment, responsibility, or kindness also have less value.

A handsome bartender who promises women nothing has far more success with beautiful women than an average looking accountant who offers his devotion. This wouldn't be the case in a world where women were primarily mothers. In that world, a woman would have to consider the possibility of pregnancy and the future of her child. But today, men who are more likely to raise a child with a woman aren't necessarily more successful in the dating market. This change in social behavior has also contributed to the increase of single mothers.

Aside from affecting the integrity of our families, feminism also has a qualitative effect on our mothers. Under feminism, an entire generation of women has been raised in the belief that being a mother is a low-status occupation. And when a person thinks something is low status, they're less likely to take it seriously. Women in traditional societies learned how to take care of children and manage a home from their mothers because they knew that one day they would have the same responsibilities. Also, schools used to teach home economics classes but have now replaced them with computer science classes. Thus, the percentage of young women today who possess basic life skills such as cooking is frighteningly low, with some proudly displaying their ignorance as a sign of liberation. Their children will have to bear the brunt of these failings in the form of unhealthy frozen food and take-out.

Feminists often hope that as more women become career-oriented, more men will choose to become stay-at-home dads. That hasn't happened. There may be a higher percentage of stay-at-home dads today than in the past, but it's still a miniscule percentage. These dads are at home largely because they can't find work or are ill, not because they want to provide childcare.[148] It's completely alien to male nature to renounce all ambition, rely on one's wife, and stay at home with the kids. A man would be ashamed of himself and no amount of socialization could persuade him otherwise. As it is, childcare will continue to largely be women's work, if only because men are much more willing to neglect their children than women are.

Teaching women that they should act like men has been a disservice to all but a tiny sliver of women. Research shows that while the representation of

---

[148] Gretchen Livingston. Growing Numbers of Dads Home with the Kids. *Pew Research Center* (June 5, 2014).

women in higher education and the professional world has risen since the 1970s, women, as a whole, today are less happy than they were then.[149] The smart and ambitious women can have all they've dreamed of, but all the other women would likely be better off in a more traditional world. These women would have married someone they met in college and then became stay-at-home moms who got to watch their children grow up. But now they must meet the social expectation of having a career and being mom. There's also a good chance they end up as single moms. Men now have trouble playing the traditional masculine role of family provider.

The family is the basic social structure of any society, and it's the result of millions of years of fine-tuning through natural selection. Social changes and advances in birth control have upended that balance. The results have been disastrous. Current data suggests that soon, most children would be born into single parent homes. It's hard to imagine what our nation would look like then.

---

[149] Betsey Stevenson and Justin Wolfers, "The Paradox of Declining Female Happiness," *American Economic Journal: Economic Policy* 1, no. 2 (August 2009), 190-225.

Is there a gender wage gap?

Many left-leaning politicians loudly proclaim that women are being paid 76% of what men are paid, and conclude there's widespread sex discrimination in the workplace.[150] That's nonsense; if that were true, then companies would just fire all their male employees and replace them with women. Corporations would instantly massively increase their profits. However, it is true that the median woman's income is about 80% of the median man's income.[151]

This is largely due to the different occupational preferences men and women have.[152] For example, women disproportionately choose lower-paying fields, such as social work or teaching, rather than higher-paying fields such as construction work or engineering. Women also tend to work fewer hours than men, often to spend more time with their children. Having a high-paying career usually requires long and unpredictable hours, as well as frequent

---

[150] Charlotte Alter, "Hillary Clinton Calls for Closing Wage Gap on Equal Pay Day, *Time* (April 12, 2016).
[151] CONSAD Research Corporation, "An Analysis of the Reasons for the Disparity in Wages Between Men and Women," U.S. Department of Labor (January 12, 2009).
[152] Catherine Hakim, "Women, Careers, and Work-Life Preferences," *British Journal of Guidance & Counselling* 34, no. 3 (August 2006), 279-294.

travel. Many more men than women are willing to accept that trade-off.

After accounting for occupational choices and hours worked, a woman who has the same job and does the same work as a man is paid, on average, 95% of what the man is paid.[153] This is not necessarily problematic because there are still qualitative differences between men and women that are difficult to quantitatively account for. Men may simply be more aggressive in how they negotiate salary increases than women.

[153] Andrew Chamberlain, "Demystifying the Gender Pay Gap," Glassdoor research report (March 2016).

Conclusion

Few things stir up as much controversy as pointing out basic differences between men and women that are grounded in biology. I believe these facts generate extreme reactions because they fundamentally challenge the worldview built by feminists and adopted by the global elite.[154] The global elite believe gender is simply a social construct and that

---

[154] The global elite are a small but influential cultural subgroup found in major cities across the world. They tend to have stellar resumes, live in major cities, travel frequently, and consume left-wing multimedia. As an illustration: think of an Ivy League educated New Yorker who reads the New York Times, watches Saturday Night Live and vacations in Nice. While their membership spans nationalities, their worldviews are remarkably homogeneous. They reject nationalism in favor of multiculturalism, gender roles in favor of feminism, and race realism in favor ridged racial sameness. This tiny section of the population controls the mass media, universities, and many elite industries. They have the power to enforce their views on the general public, even if the general public disagrees with those views. *See* Joseph King, *Awake* (2017).

there are no fundamental differences between men and women. That's a ridiculous lie that has done substantial harm to our nation.

On average, there are differences between men and women because they have faced different reproductive problems throughout their evolutionary history. Men are strong, violent, competitive, group-oriented, and have a fascination with how the natural world works. Women are empathetic, egalitarian, and have a fascination with people. Men are born to be warriors, and women are born to be mothers.

Since the dawn of civilization, men have worked hard to provide for and protect their families. When enemies were at the gates, men went forth and sacrificed their lives so their people could live on. The efforts of men ultimately led to the advanced industrialized world today, where we enjoy a degree of peace and prosperity that is without precedent. There's still crime, but imagine how treacherous the world was for a woman or child even a few hundred years ago. Back then, the king's law traveled on horseback and there weren't even phones to call for help with. Without electric streetlights, the night was truly dark and full of terrors.

Today, there is virtually no hunger in the advanced industrialized world; in fact, obesity is one of our most significant public health concerns. For most of history, people spent all their time working for food like any other animal, with starvation often just around the corner. But advances in agriculture have freed us from that burden, and most of us have enough economic freedom to pursue our interests and hobbies as if we were the nobility of old. Even someone with a minimum-wage job is able to afford enough food to become obese and occasionally take international vacations.

In this modern world, a woman doesn't need a man for support or protection. She can find work herself or, in some circumstances, live off government support. The government also offers her physical security through an extensive police force. Women played a very limited role in discovering the science, building the infrastructure, or managing the political institutions that led to the modern world. The modern world was built on the blood and sweat of men, yet women today seem to have no appreciation for the role men play in creating and sustaining it. Some feminist women even actively attack anything considered masculine. Masculine institutions, such as the military, church, and courts, have lost the respect they once commanded. Masculine ideas like competition, war, and nationalism are thought of as cruel or mean.

The media often discusses how machines have replaced humans in many manual jobs, and how artificial intelligence and robots might eventually even make cognitive-demanding jobs like doctors obsolete. But their speculation ignores a more profound and immediate social change that is occurring right before us. Men seem to have built a world in which they're no longer needed or respected. The trend appears to be towards a celebration of feminine values, and a denigration of masculine values as "toxic." But that trend belies an important truth.

The fundamental contradiction of feminism is that it can only exist with the permission and under the protection of men. Men provide physical security, technology, and legal rights that have allowed women to claim equal standing to men. Across the world and throughout history, women themselves have never been able to build a nation. Always and everywhere, women enjoy the comfort and security that men provide. Everything from the buildings women reside in, to the electricity their televisions run on, to the police force that keeps them safe come from the labors of men. Nation building requires a set of skills that women simply don't have.

Man's passion for understanding the inanimate world led to the science and technology that sustain the material comforts we enjoy. Man's inclination for hierarchy necessitated the creation of rules, and his competitive nature spurred on improvements that benefited everyone. Man's loyalty to his own group meant he was willing to protect and support his fellow citizens, and they him. Nation building is part of a Man's DNA.

Women are altogether different. A woman's beliefs are those that make her feel better, rather than those that are true. Women lack the passion for understanding the inanimate world that is necessary for advances in science and technology. Women's strong empathy precludes the rule of law, since exceptions will continually be made for those they feel sorry for. It also precludes competition and the improvements that come with it, because women wouldn't want the losers to feel bad about themselves. Most importantly, a woman's empathy also means she doesn't believe we should treat our own people better than foreigners. Unsurprisingly, women have never built a nation.

Until the very recent past, a woman's role has always been primarily that of a mother. This role has been baked into a woman's DNA, and is apparent even in toys she gravitates towards when she's a little girl. While young boys take any toy and turn it into a weapon, young girls take any toy and try to nurture it. A woman's empathy and interest in people make her a perfect fit for managing a home. This is the basic division of labor between the sexes that has been the foundation of human civilization since Adam and Eve.

Social and technological changes over the past 100 years have upended this foundation with disastrous consequences. Women now clamor for roles traditionally held by men, and men are taught that that a woman can do everything a man can. But her feminine nature is a poor fit for managing a nation. The rise of feminism has led to the decay of our families, the erosion of our culture, and the gradual disintegration of our political institutions. Men are not obsolete; they're indispensable.

It might seem that I blame the decline of our civilization on feminism, but that's not true. Walking on the streets of New York, I once saw a man wearing a shirt with the slogan, "The Future is Female." I expect women to act in accordance with their nature, but I also expect men to behave like men. Our civilization is decaying because our men have abdicated their responsibility as the architects, builders, and supporters of civilization. It is the responsibility of men to use their masculine nature to stand up to the whims of feminists. But our men have forgotten how to be men.

To be a man is to be a warrior for his tribe. Feminists suggest that our tribe is the human race, but that's the same thing as saying there's no tribe. Our nation is our tribe, and our duty is to advance its interests. That means taking actions that benefit the nation as a whole, even if it's at the expense of foreigners and minorities within our nation. That means making decisions based on the truth, even if it hurts someone's feelings. That means understanding that men and women are different, and that a woman's views aren't suited to governing a nation. Ultimately, it means taking on the mantle of leadership that has been worn by our fathers and forefathers. Men alone have always possessed both the courage and originality to change the world. As long the men stand firm, the women will follow, as they have since the dawn of time.

Early feminist Ida Tarbell clawed her way through a male-dominated world to become one of the most distinguished journalists of her generation. Later in her life, unmarried and childless, she began to re-think her views on the role of women and exhorted young women to embrace roles as mothers and homemakers. She admitted a woman "is a different being. Whether she is better or worse, stronger or weaker, primary or secondary is not the question. She is different."[155] Many career-oriented women today walk the path pioneered by Tarbell only to reach the same unhappy conclusion. Feminism gave women the freedom to behave like men, but not the wisdom or courage to acknowledge that they're not men. To move forward as a nation, we must remember and honor our past.

---

[155] Ida Tarbell, "The Uneasy Woman," *The American Magazine* 73 (1912), 261.

Joseph King

Epilogue

I began this book with a simple question: how are men and women different? What I found in part surprised me, but in part confirmed many things that I had already suspected. On average, there are meaningful differences between men and women across a wide range of attributes. These differences matter. While the 19th Amendment had little impact in the years after its passage, it has now fundamentally altered our national fabric in a way that is nothing short of revolutionary. Politics today is incomprehensible without acknowledging the existence of distinct male and female natures.

In Europe and in the U.S. there are movements towards unlimited immigration from third world countries, which amounts to the abolition of national boundaries and thus the dissolution of nations. Similar movements cannot be found in history. In history, what we see are groups of men killing and ruling over foreign groups of men. Open borders is an extreme example, but marks of the feminine nature can be seen in everywhere.

To be fair, both feminine and masculine values have their place. A ruler with no empathy degenerates into a tyrant. The perpetual warfare common in a world ruled by men is also not ideal. There is a balance that must be struck, but in the context of national affairs that balance must be tilted towards the views of men.

The 19th Amendment is etched in stone and will never be changed. But that that does not mean men cannot take back the reins of power. Feminists did not take power from men, it is men who willingly relinquished it. Men relinquished it because they were taught that women were their equals in national affairs. What is needed is for men to awaken from that delusion.

When I was in college I thought gender roles were relics from a barbaric past. That is what everyone was taught, but over time my thinking evolved with my growing life experience. As I put this book together I read widely and came in touch with the large amount of scientific work done on differences between the sexes. The more I read, the more I began to realize that what I was taught was political propaganda.

Young men today are taught the same lies, or worse. Some schools teach young men that they are bad for historically oppressing women and that masculinity is "toxic." All that damaging nonsense is also parroted in the mass media. Anyone who challenges these views is categorically dismissed. The feminists and their global elite allies unfortunately hold significant power.

But lies are always fragile, and no amount of power can turn a lie into a truth. I write this book as a public service to teach men the truths that I have learned. My hope is that this knowledge will help them make sense of the world. I hope that it will awaken them to rise up and take on their true roles as leaders, as men.

Thank you for taking the time to read my book. If you think that it has been helpful to you, please leave a review online so that others can also find it.

Joseph King

About the Author

Joseph is an attorney based in New York City. He is a graduate of Columbia University and spent over a decade abroad in East Asia and Western Europe. His passion is to speak truth to power. Please check out his other book, *Awake: An Introduction to New Nationalism.*

www.ingramcontent.com/pod-product-compliance
Lightning Source LLC
Chambersburg PA
CBHW032110280326
41933CB00009B/786